W9-BZB-613

A Daughter's Touch

A Daughter's Touch

one woman's journey
through postpartum depression

Sylvia Lasalandra

Quattro M Publishing

2005

A Daughter's Touch
Copyright © 2004 by Sylvia Lasalandra
Published by Quattro M Publishing

All rights reserved. No part of this book may be reproduced
(except for inclusion in reviews), disseminated or utilized in any form
or by any means, electronic or mechanical, including photocopying,
recording, or in any information storage and retrieval system,
or the Internet/World Wide Web without written permission
from the author or publisher.

This is a work of non-fiction, but out of respect for the privacy
of some individuals their names have been changed.

For further information, please contact the author at:
adaughterstouch@aol.com

Book design by THE FLOATING GALLERY
www.thefloatinggallery.com

Printed in the United States of America

Library of Congress Control Number 2004195528
ISBN 0-9764867-0-X

This book is dedicated to

My husband Michael, who suffered postpartum depression with me, for never giving up on me and loving me when I couldn't even love myself. It is through your love, support, and faith that I was able to conquer PPD.

My mother and father, who put their lives unselfishly on hold to save my life and the life of their granddaughter.

My daughter Melina: hand in hand we will be, forever together you and me. I love you, I love you, I love you . . .

All the women and children who are no longer here to speak because this insidious disease has taken them away too soon. I am here to be your voice.

All the women who are suffering today with PPD. Don't be afraid to ask for help. You are not alone. Together we can kick PPD's butt!

Finally, I'd like to dedicate this book to my Aunt Stella, for saving my mother's life thirty-five years ago, when she suffered PPD. I love you and miss you.

Acknowledgments

I would like to thank M.A.K. (you know who you are!) for the sacrifices that you made for me, for your undying support and pledge to keep me alive. My Aunt Lina and my cousin Anna for loving Melina as if she was their own. My incredible family; Nicky, Jimmy, Johnny, Davey, Kim and Joe for their understanding and prayers. My beautiful friend Kelly, the best friend and godmother in the world! The Amati family for making Melina laugh when I couldn't. Father Michael Carnevale, for confirming that gods love for me is unconditional. Lucy for being honest with me and the Frodella family for their love. My dear friends Janie and Donna for their patience and bringing the old Sylvia back! Chipper for truly caring and babysitting me! Ryan Keenen for being such a loyal and incredible friend! Anna and Jim C. for letting me know that the door was always open for me. Jo Jo, Karen, Keri, Ted and the entire staff at *Bruschetta* and *Bacchus*.

Karen & Dave Mason for just being who you are. Judy, Judy, Judy, you're the best!

Finally, I would like to thank my editor and friend Leigh, for her guidance and keeping me focused.

To all the people that I forgot to thank, get over it!

A Daughter's Touch

Introduction: Call Me Crazy

I looked at the digital clock on the dashboard of my car and realized I'd been in the mall parking lot for an hour and a half. I had just been sitting there — car in park, radio and ignition off — just sitting and staring. It was hot inside my navy blue sedan — the weather was unusually warm for October — and I did not smell good. Without the cool breeze of the air conditioner, beads of sweat rolled down my cheeks and the back of my neck. I watched the clock for another ten minutes before I finally peeled myself off the leather saddle upholstery. It was time to get functional.

My destination was Borders. I needed to know I was not alone in my despair and shame. Surely, I could find some books to help me understand why I was so miserable at what was supposed to be the happiest time of my life. Someone else must have experienced what was happening to me. Barely three months before, I had given birth to a perfect, beautiful baby girl and I wanted nothing to do with her. Something was wrong with me and I needed to know I wasn't the monster I saw in the mirror; that the Sylvia I knew was somewhere underneath.

Our newborn daughter, Melina, had been living at my parents' house for nearly two months and I still felt petrified. My husband, Michael, was ready to start being a father and was growing impatient. *When could our baby come home and be with us*, he wanted to know. I had no answers for him, but Melina was safe with my parents. She wasn't safe with me.

The stories of Andrea Yates haunted me: she drowned her five beautiful children in the family bathtub without explanation. Even though she had a history of mental illness, and I didn't, I could see a similar path in front of me and I was terrified nothing would stop me.

My friend Marianna, a psychologist, was trying to help. She had referred me to one colleague after another, but none of them offered any solutions. Doctors and nurses were sending me on my way with a pat on the head and a, "You'll feel better, just give it time." My symptoms and behaviors were dismissed with a pitying look and a prescription for another antidepressant or sleeping pill. I was desperate for answers and, it seemed, I would have to find them on my own.

I pulled the handle of the car door and swung my sneakered feet to the pavement. They felt heavy and unsure. Slowly, I stood up and felt the light breeze on my face. The entrance to the mall seemed so far away. I had taken the day off from the restaurant, although I wasn't getting much work done while I was there. As if on autopilot, I floated through the parking lot, past mothers with toddlers, strollers and packages in tow.

Fully functioning mothers could see, from my damp, matted hair and three-day-old jeans and T-shirt, that I was not one of them. I turned to go back to the car, but stopped. I couldn't hide there. The people in the parking lot would know what a failure I was. At the glass doors, I stood, trapped by panic, until a man with an Old Navy bag held the door open for me. I nodded my thanks, put my head down, my long, dark brown hair hiding my face, and plodded on through the shame.

The harsh fluorescent lighting burned my tired, blood-shot eyes. I could smell the aroma of coffee wafting from the café... I used to love coffee. I didn't love anything anymore. I tried to make myself invisible as I negotiated shoppers and benches and planters until I reached another set of glass doors and my possible salvation.

Wandering aimlessly through the stacks, I somehow found my way to the nonfiction floor. I scanned the shelves with growing agitation and frustration. The self-help section proved to be the opposite of its name. If I needed a husband or organizational skills or even a parachute, I would have been in luck. Unfortunately, I needed to know why I wanted to kill myself and my baby every time I closed my eyes — or opened them. I moved on to the psychology section.

Obsessive-compulsive disorder, bipolar disorder, anxiety disorder — all covered. Nothing about I-want-to-kill-my-kid disorder. Postpartum depression apparently did not exist, at least not in the world of pop psychology. I wanted to scream, "Somebody help me! Hasn't anyone else ever felt this way?" I might have actually screamed, because, suddenly, a young man came up behind me.

"May I help you find something?" he asked politely. He swept the blond hair from his eyes and put his hand in the pocket of his khaki pants.

"Yes. Would you like my kid?" I snapped. He looked at me wide-eyed and stunned, his mouth slightly agape. "Actually, I am looking for some books on postpartum depression."

"Hmmm." He looked at me quizzically. "Let's look at the

3

computer and see what we can find." I shuffled my feet along the green carpet, following him to a computer terminal a few feet away. He typed on the keyboard, hit 'enter' and looked up with a smile. "I'm sure we have something for you."

I tried to return his smile, but the most I could muster was a moment's eye contact. I looked back down at my dirty jeans and regretted my decision to forego a bath that morning. Hygiene had not been a high priority of late, but I was doing better. I had actually brushed my teeth before I left the house. Baby steps.

"Here we are," blond-clerk-boy chirped. "We have two titles dealing with postpartum depression."

"Only two?" I asked. I was shocked. With a new psychological disorder on the news every day, how could there only be two books on postpartum? "What are they?"

"*Behind the Smile*, by Marie Osmond,..."

Great, I thought, *a celebrity autobiography*. No offense to Marie Osmond, but how deep is someone in the public eye really going to delve?

"... and *Maternal Brain: Neurological Neurobiologic Neuro-endocrine Adaptation and Disorders in Pregnancy and Post-Partum* by J.A. Russell, et al."

"What? Are you kidding me? That's it?" I couldn't believe it: a celebrity fluff piece and an academic journal. Maybe I really was the only one going through this.

"No, ma'am. That's all we have. I can show you where they are, if you like." The clerk was trying so hard to be helpful, even as he looked at me like I might go postal.

"Yes, thank you," I replied. I could at least give them a chance. "Maybe Marie really can help me. I grew up watching her ice-skate... we were practically best friends. And

J.A. Russell? Well, he may talk big, but he probably has some very pertinent information."

The blond clerk just looked at me. Sarcasm was, apparently, not his bag.

"This way," he said, indicating with his hand. He guided me through the psychology section. "Here's *Maternal Brain*." He handed me the plain, blue paperback with black, straightforward lettering. I opened it and peeked at the first page. I was in for a treat.

"This way." The clerk and I pressed on to biography. "Here we are: Marie Osmond." He handed me the glossy paperback with a plastically smiling Marie on the cover. Behind the Smile . . . *At least she can smile*, I thought. And then I tried — and failed.

"Thank you for your help." I tried to sound sincere.

"You're welcome, ma'am. Have a good day." The clerk cheerfully waved me off and went back to his post at the computer terminal.

Still in shock, I walked to the cashier. I was about to leave one of the largest, most well-stocked bookstores in the country with only slightly more information than I had when I came in. Where were the stories of real women who have gone through PPD? Not to discount Marie Osmond's experience and struggle, but she's not exactly a working class girl from New Jersey. A millionaire with a millionaire's resources is going to deal with crises very differently from the rest of us. I read the first few pages of *Maternal Brain* while I waited in line. I had no idea what I was reading. If I was a doctor, maybe I would get it, but I was already on the brink and this thing just might send me over.

"Next," the cashier called out.

"I'll take this one," I said, handing her the Marie Osmond book, "and you can keep this fucking thing," dropping J.A. Russell, et al. on the counter.

"Okay . . ." The cashier blinked at me.

I knew in my heart there had to be others who had suffered with this disease, but no one seemed to be talking about it. After months of pain and frustration, I was learning that postpartum depression was a closely guarded secret. I decided at that moment, there in the Borders checkout line, that I was going to find out why, and when I did, I was going to tell everybody.

Wedding Day, 1993:
with Davey, Nicky, me, Jimmy and Johnny

One

Raise a Glass

Postpartum depression can happen to anyone, regardless of age, economics, race or parental status.

The Frodella family was gathered around my mother-in-law's mahogany dining room table for the traditional Thanksgiving meal. Michael's mom and sister, Lucy, always set a beautiful table, bringing out the Italian linen tablecloth and the good china for any special gathering. Michael and I arrived after spending the afternoon with my folks, joining Michael's very warm and populous family. We ate and laughed with the usual gusto, keeping an eye on the football game in progress in the adjoining TV room.

Before the end of the meal, Mom and Pops brought out a decanter of their legendary homemade wine. It was delicious, and so strong. I had had at least two glasses when Michael's mother started teasing me.

"Be careful, Sylvia," she laughed. "When I was younger, every time I drank my holiday wine, I got pregnant!" Everyone laughed and, football suddenly forgotten, all eyes were on me. In an Italian family, babies take precedence over sports. I swallowed hard, thinking of Michael's seven siblings.

"Drink a gallon," Pops chuckled. "Maybe you'll have twins!"

"Very funny," I laughed.

"Hey, it's no joke," he continued. "Frodellas don't shoot blanks."

Michael and I had been married for seven years. We wanted to have a family, but we were in no hurry. Career had always come first. Having both been raised in pizzerias, Michael and I knew the business well, and so we opened and ran a very successful, upscale Italian restaurant, *Bruschetta*, and we were about to begin another venture, to be called *Bacchus*. Our parents had always been supportive of our choice to postpone having kids, although we were pretty sure they were concocting a secret, pro-grandchild plan behind our backs. Maybe this was it.

We laughed and joked about Frodellas yet to be, but inside, my heart pounded with anticipation. Though we had told no one, Michael and I had just decided to start trying to have a baby. The coincidence was not so shocking, but it threw me for a bit of a loop. I tried to put it out of my head. Homemade wine or not, there was no way I was going to get pregnant just like that. The decision had been made, but I wasn't 22 anymore, and, in my mind, it was still a concept for the future.

A couple of weeks later, I met my good friend Marianna for coffee. We had been going around and around for at least ten minutes and I was getting exasperated with her. My period, while right on time, had started and then stopped abruptly — and Marianna had a theory.

"Marianna, there is no way I'm pregnant," I insisted, taking another sip of my coffee. The café teemed with people and our heated debate was absorbed in the din of customers, servers and clattering coffee cups and saucers.

"Sylvia, that would explain the fatigue, the lack of concentration," she persisted, brushing her blond bangs out of her eyes. "You have to listen to what your body is telling you."

"I'm just working too hard. I'm at the restaurant day and night — and so is Michael. There is no way his little swimmers are up to the task."

"Whatever you say," she laughed. "But it's worth checking out."

It made no sense. We had only had sex once since Thanksgiving — that very night, as a matter of fact. It went against everything I had read about conceiving after age 30. Of course, I knew that it was possible, but it just didn't seem probable. I put my white ceramic cup on its saucer and impatiently stirred the dregs with my spoon.

"Fine. I'll do a test."

"Today," Marianna insisted. She stood up from the table and threw her black leather coat over her shoulders. "Call me as soon as you know." She waved for the waitress and hugged me tightly. "Bye, girl."

"Ciao, baby." I waved as she bounced to the door.

The waitress brought the check and I sat for another few minutes with Marianna's words swimming in my head. She was right; I should find out. I dug into my purse, put down some money for the bill and slipped on my puffy, black winter coat. I had a couple of hours before they needed me at the restaurant. It was as good a time as any.

As I drove to the drug store near our house, fantasies

11

about being a mother danced in my head. I always thought I would have children, but it always seemed like something that would happen later, in the future.

I made my way through the long aisles of the store. The "Family Planning" aisle was at the back, near the pharmacy. I stood for about five minutes, overwhelmed by my choices in home pregnancy detection. One of them was marked "Buy one, get one free." *Two opinions are better than one*, I figured, and took my selection to the counter.

Michael had already gone to *Bruschetta* to begin the dinner prep, so I had the house to myself. I crossed the threshold of our little dollhouse and put my purse on the table by the door. I tossed my coat onto the purple chaise in the living room and, taking the package from the shopping bag, I walked up the stairs to the bathroom, reading the box as I climbed. The instructions seemed simple enough. *How hard is it to pee on a stick?* I stood by the sink and looked in the mirror. *I don't look like a mother,* I thought. *Or maybe this is what a mother looks like.* I took a deep breath and let out a sigh. *Well, I might as well get it over with.* I opened the package and, though I was alone in the house, I closed the door.

When I was finished, I put the indicator stick on the edge of the sink and watched it. Nothing was happening, so I walked down the short hallway to our bedroom and began dressing for work. *There is so much to do*, I scolded myself. *Why did I waste the time to take this stupid test? I know my body; I should know if I'm pregnant.* I put on my black jacket and pants, my favorite black, high-heeled boots and opened the jewelry box on the dresser.

My reflection in the dresser-top mirror seemed different somehow. I stared at myself for a minute, quizzically inspecting every line, every pore. I was exactly who I wanted to be — successful businesswoman, loving wife, dutiful daughter, trusted friend. Maybe devoted mother would be added to the list. I was happy with my life. Was it possible to be happier?

As I slid on my silver bangle bracelet, I saw the clock on the nightstand.

"Shit, I'm going to be late!" I said to no one — not that anyone would be surprised at my tardiness. With all my good points, I had my flaws as well.

I ran down the stairs, picked up my coat, grabbed my purse from the table and rushed out the door to the car. Sinking down into the driver's seat, I turned the key in the ignition and backed out of the driveway. All of a sudden, in the middle of the street, I remembered the stick lying on the bathroom sink.

"Shit. I forgot the damn test."

I swung the car back into the driveway and jumped out, leaving the car running, keys dangling from the switch. Careful of the ice, I gingerly hopped up the few steps into the house, then sprinted up the stairs to the bathroom. Through the open door, I could see from the hall the bright blue plus sign blazing at me.

"What? No way!"

I stood in the doorframe and stared it down, like a spider in the corner. *Okay,* I thought. *How accurate can these things be? Maybe I did it wrong. Maybe I peed too much.* I galloped back downstairs and outside to turn off the car. I was certainly getting my exercise.

Once again, upstairs I went, and, without taking off my

coat, I took the second test from the package, dropped my pants and gave a couple of drops to the little window. This time I held it in my hand and watched. The seconds ticked by tortuously as I waited, but I couldn't take my eyes off it. Slowly, there began to appear a blue plus sign in the indicator window. *Unbelievable,* I thought. *This is unbelievable. Who gets pregnant from one try?*

It took several minutes for reality to sink in. I was pregnant. I was going to be a mother. Michael was going to be a father. We would be a family. *Michael! I have to call Michael.* The bedroom phone was in my hand before I knew what was happening.

"Mike, it's Sylvia." I sunk down onto the bed. "You are never going to believe this."

I drove all the way to the restaurant with the thing on the seat next to me. I called my mother from my cell phone. She cried happy tears, singing praises to God in Italian. Although it was hard to wrap my mind around the idea, I was happy, too. *I'm so young. Too young.* But I wasn't. I was 32. It was time. It was exactly the right time.

Marianna was next on the call list. As I pulled into the parking lot of *Bruschetta*, she congratulated me.

"Wow, that's wonderful! That explains all the tiredness. Oh, Syl, I'm so happy for you."

"I know. I'm so relieved to know. God bless your intuition," I laughed. "I'm here. I gotta go see Michael."

The restaurant was a bustle of activity. The dinner crowd was coming in, so I entered through the side door that led to the kitchen. Michael, as head chef, was on the line, preparing meals for our hungry customers. The kitchen staff scurried about in controlled chaos. Michael must have had one eye on the door because, as soon as I entered, he dropped his tongs and ran over to me.

"Hey, girl." He looked into my eyes and smiled at me with excitement and anticipation, waiting for me to confirm what he already knew.

"Hi," I smiled back. We just stood there for a second, like the calm center of a storm, before we embraced. He bent down and hugged me tightly, righted himself and pulled my feet from the floor.

"I'm so happy," he whispered in my ear. "Are you sure?"

"I'm sure."

"I love you," he breathed.

"I love you, too."

Michael and I did our best to keep things professional at work. We were casual and friendly with our staff, but we rarely showed affection in public and tried to keep our personal lives confined to our home. We had a rule to never bring work home and vice versa. Seeing us hug in the middle of the dinner rush, everyone knew something was up. Michael put me down and, still holding my hand, turned and cleared his throat.

"Hey, everybody, Sylvia has some news." Michael's voice echoed through the kitchen, grabbing everyone's attention.

"We're going to have a baby," I happily announced. I was still reeling from the news myself, but these people were my family, and I was thrilled to share our joy with them.

Congratulations volleyed like Ping-Pong balls. "Sylvia!" Ryan, our young general manager, yelled out above the rest. "Oh, my God!" He hugged me tightly, almost knocking the wind out of me. "I'm so happy for you."

I was elated, yet overwhelmed and a little dizzy. Michael received pats on the back from the sous chefs and prep guys. I felt like I was in a receiving line — everyone wanted to hug the new mom.

Jo Jo, our bar manager, burst into the kitchen. "What is going on in here?" she shouted in her raspy smoker's voice. "You're having a party, and I wasn't invited?"

"Michael and Sylvia are having a baby!" Ryan squealed.

"Wow! That's great!" Jo Jo ran over to hug me. "Hey, Roger is in the bar. You better tell him before he hears it through the grapevine."

"Since it's already out, you might as well make it official," Ryan said. "Come on, you two." He took both our hands in his and led us out through the swinging door into the crowded bar. Jo Jo followed, lighting up a cigarette. "May I have your attention, please?" Ryan bellowed.

Gradually, conversations abated and an odd kind of quiet settled in. The bar opened into the plush, warmly lit dining room, both filled to capacity. Every eye was on us.

"Michael and Sylvia have an announcement," Ryan said, giving us the floor. I was the face of *Bruschetta*. I knew each and every one of my customers, and I treated them all like family. Hell, they were family. I fed them. I was a mother already. I smiled confidently and took center stage.

"Hi, everyone," I paused for dramatic effect, making eye contact with as many people as I could, surveying my domain. I know how to work a room; I'm really an actress at heart. "I know you all thought the day would never come, but it has. We are having a baby!"

I was not prepared for the magnitude of cheers that rose up from our patrons. It was like the Fourth of July. The oohs and ahs and wows nearly bowled me over. Roger, a loyal customer and friend, stood up from his customary corner stool and raised his hand.

"This is a special day. We need champagne!" He called for a bottle of Dom Perignon.

Jo Jo was quick on her feet and, before I knew it, Michael and some of the staff hoisted glasses of champagne. I, of course, had a ginger ale.

"A toast," Roger continued. "A toast to Sylvia and Michael. May your lives be blessed with the joys only children can bring."

The cheers to our health and happiness echoed throughout the restaurant, as people stood and applauded our happy news. The kitchen had come to a standstill and the staff gathered in the doorway, whistling and clapping. My life had been pretty close to perfect up to that moment, and yet I felt a surge of joy that I had not experienced before nor expected. The next chapter of my life was beginning, and I was ready to savor it.

Two

An Unexpected Reality

Making the decision to have a child — it's momentous. It is to decide forever to have your heart go walking outside your body.

—Elizabeth Stone, writer

During the first trimester of my pregnancy, I tried to carry on as if nothing was different. *Bruschetta* was thriving and we were close to finding a location for our new venture, a wine bar and chop house we would call *Bacchus*. Running a restaurant is grueling work — long hours and late nights are par for the course. I handled the business and front of house aspects of *Bruschetta* and was busy making preparations for the new restaurant. Michael, as executive chef for both, was working more than I was. There was little time for rest, with or without our newly pregnant situation.

The euphoria of the first weeks had waned and the reality of impending parenthood was setting in. Life was going on as normal, but what I knew to be normal was already beginning to change. The usual physical transformations had started, but in my mind, it still seemed impossible that we

19

were really going to have a baby. She wasn't a "she" yet, kind of a conceptual baby, an idea that had yet to become a reality. We were happy about the possibility of "It," but, at least in my case, "It" was still just an idea, and "It" was getting in my way.

A major winter storm blanketed the northeast in mid February of 2000 and dumped two feet of snow on our little house in New Jersey. I was in the habit of doing some of my work from home and then going to the restaurant in the afternoon. Already dark at 4 p.m., I bundled up and trudged out to my car sitting in the driveway, which was immobilized due to the ice and snow. Michael had gone in long before me and I was alone. I knew I should not be doing anything as strenuous as shoveling the driveway, but I had to get to work. *Nothing's ever stopped me from shoveling snow before*, I thought. *Why should I let this baby — this nonperson that I don't even know — keep me from doing what I have to do?* The rationalization seemed logical enough at the time. I charged back through the house into the shed, grabbed the shovel and went to it. It was a heavy, wet snow that had turned quickly to ice. I poked and scraped and dug my way through with all my strength. I may be petite, but I'm strong. It took about half an hour to clear the walk and the driveway enough to be passable. *That wasn't so hard*, I thought, as I went back inside.

I was hot and sweaty under my heavy coat and gloves. Peeling off the layers of outerwear, I went into the kitchen to have a glass of water and then upstairs to change for work. I went to the bathroom and, to my horror, found I was spotting. *What have I done?* I'd wished for "It" to just go away on a couple of occasions, and now I had done it. I had killed "It."

I ran to the phone and called Dr. Tebbe, my OB/GYN,

but she was out of the office. One of her partners, Dr. Weiss, took the call. He told me to calm down, though not before he scolded me for doing something so dangerous, and to put my feet up. Water and rest was his prescription, and if the bleeding didn't stop in a couple of hours, I was to report to the emergency room. In a panic, I did what I was told. *How could I be so stupid?* Of course, I didn't really want my baby to die, I just wanted things to continue as normal. I had not accepted that my life would be forever altered by our decision to start a family. I propped my feet up on the couch with pillows and called my mother.

"Are you crazy?" she screamed and cursed me in Italian. "You should have your fat ass on the couch and be watching TV." That set me off more than the well-deserved reprimand.

"Hey, I'm only three months," I yelled back. "I am not fat!"

I did what I was told and, by that evening, the spotting had stopped. My next checkup revealed that, much to my relief, everything was fine, but my "bad behavior" didn't stop there. I continued to haul the laundry up a flight of stairs from our laundry room to our bedroom. At work, I carried cases of wine up from the cellar without even thinking. A difficult job for anyone — a case generally holds from six to twelve bottles — there I was, all 5 feet, 110 pounds of me, trudging up the steps to restock the bar. My coworkers would yell at me if they caught me, but I paid no attention.

I had been doing everything else right. For all my conflicted feelings about having a kid, an urge to protect the health of my unborn child prevailed in other ways. I stopped drinking alcohol — no small feat for a wine lover like me; I joined a spa with a pool and swam several times a week; I walked quite often, taking strolls around the neighborhood to stay in shape. Being in the restaurant biz, Michael always made sure that I ate well and, except for work, I managed to keep stress to a minimum. This healthy behavior just didn't jibe with my occasional reckless excursions.

For some reason, it was okay if I did something stupid that would kill the baby, but anything that would cause long-term damage or that would produce an unhealthy child was unthinkable. Luckily, that rationale changed when I went for my second sonogram. Suddenly, the imaginary baby became a reality.

Michael, my parents and I went to the obstetrician's office together. The first sonogram had been uneventful; the baby was just a little speck, a tiny pea that Dr. Tebbe swore would eventually look like a kid. This was the big one. I was five and a half months pregnant and we were about to find out the gender of our child.

I lay on the exam table with my shirt hiked up over my protruding belly. Dr. Tebbe squirted a cold gel onto my stomach and slowly massaged it with the wand-thingy. A female technician adjusted knobs and dials on the ultrasound machine. I tried to lie still, even though it tickled. My family gathered around the screen awaiting the first real glimpse of our baby.

"Sylvia, can you see it?" the doctor asked me. She pointed to the screen as I craned my neck around for a peek. "There's an arm... and here... that's the torso... and here's the head." I gasped at the sight. It did look like a real kid, with arms and legs and eyes; a perfect little baby. My heart pounded, and Michael squeezed my hand.

"Is it a boy or a girl?" he asked. It was not obvious to the untrained eye from the cloudy image.

"Are you sure you want to know?" Dr. Tebbe asked.

"We're sure," I insisted. I needed to know. I needed it to be real.

"You are having a baby girl."

Wow. A girl. I didn't know how to react. I had secretly wanted a boy. In my mind, it seemed that having a boy would somehow be easier. I wasn't disappointed, but I felt strange and unsure. Then I looked at my parents. Tears streamed down my father's face, something I had rarely seen in my life. He was from the heel of the boot, Southern Italy, where men don't cry. My little Sicilian mother smiled with joyful tears in her eyes and, to this day, I am filled with pride and a profound happiness when I recall the moment.

"Sylvia," she leaned in, "a daughter is very special. You are my pillar of strength, and now you have yours."

After all those years of feeling lost in the crowd of brothers, I knew the secret. Mothers and daughters have a very special bond, not just with each other, but with the whole family. They hold everything together by holding up one another. I was about to add another link to the chain of strength and security that makes a family. Michael kissed my forehead and, for the first time in my pregnancy, I felt like a mom. This baby girl needed me to be strong and take good care of her and, someday, she would do the same for me.

Three

Back to Business

Major life changes, such as a move or a new career, can increase
one's chances of developing postpartum depression.

With a healthy prognosis, and feeling comforted by the
little sonogram photo I carried in my purse, I was
feeling more like my old self. I was laughing again, playing
jokes on my staff and having fun with my family and girlfriends. The relief of being past the first trimester hurdle also
allowed me to focus my attention guiltlessly on our plans for
Bacchus.

About two weeks after the ultrasound, we were to close on
a perfect space, a former Mexican restaurant. The building
needed to be gutted, but the location was perfect, not 200 feet
from *Bruschetta,* and we were sold.

The baby was due in late August and we had a lot of work
to do if we wanted to have the restaurant up and running
before she came. I was concerned that I would run out of
steam before we finished the project, and I still needed time
to prepare for being a mom. A different kind of clock was
ticking.

We were handling the design of the restaurant ourselves. With our years of experience as restaurateurs, we knew exactly what we needed to repeat our past success. I had a million ideas for the look of *Bacchus* and every detail had to be considered, from the lighting and flooring, to the chairs and silverware. Everything had to be perfect. I expected nothing less from myself or those around me. Before we even closed on the space, we spent hours with contractors, architects, electricians, painters and the like. The only roadblock was the owner of the building we planned to purchase.

We had been to countless meetings with our attorneys and, at first, everything about the sale went smoothly. They were selling us the building and the kitchen equipment as part of the deal. We had been given a couple of tours and the real estate agent provided us with photos for reference. It was exactly what we wanted. We hoped to start construction in May, but suddenly, toward the end of April, when we tried to go back and look at the space, we were refused entry. The workers would make excuses about the power or keys, until one day they just flat out said we were not allowed in until the sale was completed. I knew something was fishy, but we proceeded with negotiations anyway. About a week before the closing, it hit me — they were removing the kitchen equipment. Michael thought the same thing.

"That's why they won't let us in," I told him. "I mean, all we have to work with are these pictures, and who knows if they're still accurate."

"Look, just let the lawyers handle it. That's their job."

"But, Michael, they're ripping us off."

"Sylvia, please don't do anything crazy."

Michael knew me too well. I was not going to just stand

around and wait for someone else to do a job I could easily do myself, so I took matters into my own hands. The day before the closing, I followed my gut, which was getting bigger by the minute. I called our attorney, Marci.

"I need you to drive me over to the new restaurant."

"Okay," she said. "But why?"

"I don't want them to see my car parked outside, and they don't know yours."

"Syl, what are you getting me into?" Marci was not only one of my good friends and our lawyer, she was the town prosecutor and the wife of a police officer.

"Nothing," I lied. "I just need to check out the kitchen. They're going to let me in or I am going to break in."

"Of course you are," she sighed. There was no stopping me once I set my mind to something.

"I just need to see what they've done to it and take some pictures. It'll only take a few minutes. Can you be here in half an hour?"

"I'll be there," she relented.

My heart pounded as we pulled up in front of the former *El Bandito. Fitting,* I thought. A pregnant woman dressed all in black and an attorney in a blue power suit tiptoed around as stealthily as possible in broad daylight to the side entrance. Miracle of miracles, the door was open just a crack. Suddenly, the grinding of tires on gravel sent my heart on a free fall to my toes as a police car pulled up beside us. Like a deer in headlights, I stared at the car, caught, unable to breathe. The officer laughingly gave us a wave and I let out a shriek of relief. It was Marci's husband. Who knew it was going to be this easy? We waved back, and Marci and I crept inside. I flipped on the light.

My gut was right! The equipment we were about to pay for was gone and had been replaced with crap. Where there had once been an industrial-sized refrigerator and a six-burner gas stove, there was a regular household fridge and a tiny electric range. *No wonder they wouldn't let us in.* I got out my camera and snapped away. *They are not going to get away with this*, I thought, smiling proudly at my investigatory prowess. Mission accomplished, we dashed back to our getaway car.

The next day, Michael and I strutted into the meeting with the seller and his attorneys.

"So, I assume we're hear to discuss a new price for the property — a significantly lower price," I said cryptically.

"What?" The attorney for the sellers looked at me like I was crazy. "Why would we do that?"

"Because your client has been ripping us off." I felt like I was on *Law & Order*.

"What?"

"They've removed all the equipment from the kitchen and replaced it with shit."

"How dare you accuse my clients of cheating you?"

"Well, they won't let us in. We haven't seen inside the place in weeks. How do we know it's not true?" I was waiting for just the right moment to play my hand.

"My clients came here to settle this matter in good faith and you accuse them of theft and fraud with no basis? We don't have to listen to this." He started to pack up his papers.

"Well, perhaps you'd like proof." I smiled and reached into my folder. "These are the photos your client provided to the Realtor when we began negotiations." I lay the glossy snaps on the table in front of them. "And these," I paused, taking out a packet from the one-hour photo shop near our house, "are the photos I took yesterday."

The attorney and his clients went pale. "H-H-How did you get these?" he stammered.

"I don't think that really matters at this point, do you?"

"Well, uh, excuse me." He left the room with his clients. I looked down at my "gut" and gave her a little pat. "Good girl," I whispered.

Day to day operations at *Bruschetta* continued as usual, but I was starting to experience sudden mood swings and exhibit erratic behavior. Work that I normally enjoyed was becoming a chore, and people were getting under my skin. I had always been the fun-loving boss, easy-going Sylvia who works hard, but who knows how to have a good time.

I chalked the changes up to hormones. I certainly didn't feel like myself. Normally very focused, I would catch myself staring out of the big window at a stand of trees. When I was able to work, I was often on edge and the littlest things set me off. *If we can just get this restaurant open before the baby gets here, everything will be fine*, I told myself, but the pressure was getting to me.

One afternoon, I was sitting at my huge cherry desk at the restaurant going over invoices from our purveyors. It was the last thing I needed to do before heading over to *Bacchus* to meet with the electrician. Ted, our lovable assistant manager and resident computer guy, was sitting at his desk behind me. He had just installed a new laser printer for me, but it didn't seem to be working. I checked all the connections and made sure it was hooked up. It had worked earlier in the day, but every time I clicked "print" — nothing.

"I just want to print these fucking checks so I can get out of here!" I yelled at the machine, giving it a sound bang with my fist. I tried again. Nothing. "Enough of this shit."

Instead of asking Ted, sitting right there, for help, I leaped up in a rage. I yanked the power cord from the wall, the cable from the computer and picked up the offending contraption. I walked out of my office into the hall and, without looking to see if anyone was there, flung the printer down the stairs. I missed sending Ryan down with it by inches. The closed door at the bottom of the stairs kept the thing from crashing into the dining room, but it did not stifle the noise. Ryan looked stunned, as if he didn't know whether to hit me or hug me. He had noticed the change in my personality and had even mentioned it to Michael.

"Syl, are you okay?

"I'm fine. The printer just pissed me off." I felt terrible, but I couldn't defend myself. I couldn't even apologize. Embarrassed, I walked back into my office as if nothing happened. Ryan picked up the printer from its resting place at the bottom of the stairs and followed me back into the office.

Ted was still sitting at his desk, equally as stunned as Ryan. Ryan and Ted exchanged a flabbergasted look. The room was filled with an awkward, heavy silence. Nobody knew how to act around me anymore. The jokester, the fun, crazy Sylvia, was only making intermittent appearances. I took my place at my desk, went back to what I was doing and printed the checks with the old printer.

"Sylvia," Ryan tentatively ventured, breaking the silence, "are you feeling alright?"

"Are you a doctor?" I snapped, taking the checks and walking out the door. I did, eventually, apologize for almost killing Ryan. He was understanding and let me know that he was there for me. I felt like I had two personalities, and I really just wanted the one.

About six weeks before my due date, I went to the doctor for a checkup. It was a Friday, and Dr. Tebbe had already gone to Florida. She would return to assist Dr. Weiss perform my C-section at the end of August, as promised. Dr. Weiss was also out that day, so their third partner, Dr. Kingman, saw me. He was not my favorite — no bedside manner and no sense of humor. It was supposed to be a routine ultrasound, just to make sure everything was on track. I was lying on the exam table with my elephantine stomach exposed. Dr. Kingman stared at the screen as his assistant massaged my protrusion with the wand-thingy.

"Hmm . . . baby's head seems awfully small," he said with graveness in his voice.

"What?" I asked, stunned, trying to sit up and see the screen.

"It seems too small for her body. I don't think it's growing at a proper rate."

"But everything was fine last time I was here." My voice reflected the panic in my tightening chest.

"Well, these things can happen," he said unreassuringly.

"What things? What is wrong with my baby?"

"Well, it's hard to tell from just the ultrasound. Why don't you come back on Monday and we'll run some tests to see if the head is the right size."

"What then? What if it's not?" I felt like jumping out of my skin.

"We can either induce labor so she can continue to grow in the incubator until her head is the right size or go ahead and wait it out until your due date and do the C-section as scheduled."

"Oh my God!" I couldn't believe what was happening. "Everything was fine an hour ago."

"Go home and get some rest over the weekend, Ms. Lasalandra, and I'll see you on Monday." And with that, he stood up, gave me a quick nod of the head and left the room. The nurse smiled at me reassuringly, helping me up from the exam table.

"Don't worry," she said. "Everything will be fine."

I was wracked with guilt for the entire weekend. I was sure all of my first trimester antics had caught up with me and caused my baby to be deformed. I had given her the *mal'occhio* — the evil eye. How could I be so stupid and selfish? I prayed and prayed that everything would be fine, making deals with God for her health and protection.

My mother and Michael reassured me that I was not to blame for whatever was wrong with the baby, but they could not ease my panic and fear. The pregnancy had been going so smoothly, how could this happen? I tried to focus on getting *Bacchus* ready, and not my first horrible missteps as a mother.

Marianna and our friend Anna went with me for a more detailed color sonogram on Monday. The nurse called my name and the three of us crossed the waiting room with nervous anticipation. Dr. Medlin, a pleasant, female doctor greeted us with a smile. She explained that this kind of sonogram would show the baby in color and in greater detail so she could determine if there was a problem.

As she and the nurse prepared me for the procedure, my heart pounded. I prayed under my breath that everything would be okay and that my baby would be healthy. I never wanted anything more in my life. Anna and Marianna held my hands.

"Everything seems to be fine, Sylvia," Dr. Medlin said. "She's just small. Her head is growing at the proper rate. I don't know what Dr. Kingman was looking at, but your baby is fine."

"Are you sure? Dr. Kingman said . . ."

"She's fine," she interrupted me. "You are a small woman; you are going to have a small baby. Don't worry anymore about it. Go home and get some rest."

"Thank you." I think I breathed for the first time since we arrived. "I will." I wasn't a bad mother after all. Everything was going to be fine.

"Oh, Syl, I'm so relieved," Anna sighed. I could see the relief wash over their faces. Anna jumped up and hugged me. Marianna kissed my forehead and gave me a wink.

"Me, too," I breathed. "But remind me to kick Dr. Kingman in the balls next time I see him."

Michael and Melina

Four

Ready or Not

Your baby's first cry is the one you hear in the delivery room,
the triumphant, tension-shattering sound that says, "I'm here.
I'm breathing, I'm alive!

    —Katherine Karlsud, physician and writer.

My scheduled C-section was two weeks away and there was still so much to be done to open the restaurant. We were way behind schedule and I still had another business to run in the meantime. Michael and I were both working 70-hour weeks. With so much to do for the restaurants, there was little time for reading about pregnancy and motherhood, and there was certainly no time for nesting.

Other than enjoying the odd home improvement project, I was never particularly domestic, at least not in the traditional way. I did convert our spare room into a nursery, and that was something I was really proud of. On one of my few free days, I painted a beautiful peachy-beige faux finish on the walls that looked like Tuscan plaster, and the oak furniture had all been painted with a whitewash. I swelled a little every time I peeked in. It was exactly how I imagined it would be. She was going to love it.

Clothing and accessories had been purchased and the house had been baby-proofed. According to Sicilian superstition, the crib would be assembled and put into the nursery only after the baby was born. It seemed to me we were ready, but as we all know, life has a way of proving us wrong.

My big belly and I sat on an upside-down five-gallon bucket among the paint cans in the empty wine room at *Bacchus*, stirring a gallon of Sedona Red latex paint. The cement floor was covered with drop cloths, a ladder was propped up against the wall and a light breeze from the open windows near the ceiling wafted around the room. I was grateful for the breeze; it was another August scorcher and I was hot and uncomfortable. *Two more weeks . . . Just two more weeks.*

Though I was alone in the wine room, the restaurant was crawling with contractors and electricians. I could hear them knocking and banging around, and I knew I could call them if I needed help of any kind. The paint poured smoothly from the can into the roller pan. I enjoyed painting; it was almost meditative, and I appreciated the time alone. It also got me out of the office. There was only so much sitting I could take, even in my advanced state of pregnancy. I couldn't bear to be idle. Glowing or not, I felt so unattractive and disgusting, I relished the knowledge that I could still be useful. I never understood women who said pregnancy was beautiful. I felt ugly, fat and sluggish, but mostly like shit. The romanticism was lost on me.

I picked up the roller and submerged it in the paint, dragging it back and forth along the ridges of the pan. Twisting it around to catch a drip, I applied the red goo to the wall in thick, curving strokes. Up and down, up and down. The baby would be here soon and my whole life would be different. Would I be a good mother? Given the way I had been feeling, it seemed unlikely. Fear was creeping in and I was afraid to tell anyone. *Nothing scares Sylvia. She can do anything.* That's what people said about me. How could I tell them they were wrong?

Methodically, I worked my way around the room, up and down the ladder. When the painting was done, I began assembling the wine shelves. People thought I was crazy to keep working at this pace, but it was the only thing keeping me going. I was afraid to think about the changes that were on the way. As long as I kept busy, I wouldn't worry about the future. The unknown is frightening, but so is the realization that you are responsible for another human life. Michael and I did not think this through.

Glancing at my watch, I put down my tools and scurried to clean up and get out of there. Marianna would be at my house in two hours, and I was a mess of paint and sweat and in desperate need of a shower.

Ma came to drive me home and wait with me for Marianna to come. During the twenty-minute ride in my mother's big, comfy, lamb's wool-covered front seat, I felt oddly agitated and my stomach was queasy. So much had been done at work, but I felt restless and impatient, rather than relieved. Ma sensed that I would have the baby sooner than the scheduled due date, but she kept this premonition to herself. Twice,

I almost called Marianna to cancel our movie date, but I had been really looking forward to it. These times would be harder to come by once the baby came, so I decided to relax and enjoy it.

Ma pulled the car into the driveway, slipped it into park and came around to help me out of the car. I swung my legs around, put my feet on the pavement and heaved my huge stomach out of the car. I couldn't believe what a mountain it was. I was almost as wide as I was tall. *I'll be back to my old self soon*, I thought, *once this thing is out of me.*

Showered and freshly dressed in my favorite black Motherhood T-shirt and black leggings (They say black makes you look skinny. Ha!) I settled onto the green leather couch in the TV room and waited for Marianna. I must have dozed off, because the doorbell startled me.

"It's open," I yelled, eyes still closed. The door opened and Marianna's head peeked though the entryway. She saw me pulling myself up from my reclining position.

"Wake up, sleepy head."

"I'm awake," I said, rubbing my eyes. "Here, let me take the food into the kitchen."

"I've got it. You sit." She made her way to the kitchen. "You work too hard, Syl. You know you should be taking it easy now."

"We have been through this and through this," I sighed. "I'm fine." I started to get up to help. Marianna scolded me from the other room.

"Stay. I can do this by myself. God. Would you let someone wait on you for once?"

Marianna reappeared, put plates of food on the cocktail table and put in the video.

"Here we go," she said, relaxing onto the love seat. "A feast for queens."

For the next couple of hours, we gorged on take-out and ice cream while we laughed and cried over *The Green Mile*. Perhaps a less tearjerking movie would have been a better choice, given my hormonally driven propensity for tears, but it was nice to have my friend over, and I was sad to see it end. Michael came in from a long day at the restaurant a little before 11.

"Hello, ladies. How was your movie?" Michael leaned over me and kissed my forehead.

"Good," I sniffed. *Damn Stephen King.*

"Mind if I put the game on?" he asked.

"No. Go ahead."

"Well, sweetheart, I've got to get home," said Marianna, getting up from the love seat. I told Chip I'd be home around 11." She looked at her watch. "Oops. She smiled. "Call me if you need anything, okay?"

"Okay. I'll be fine. Drive safe."

"And call me if the baby comes," Marianna laughed.

"Yeah, right. I'll have her call you."

"Bye, Michael. Bye, bella." Marianna waved, laughing, and closed the door behind her. I got up from the sofa and padded into the kitchen. There was leftover ice cream with my name on it. I heard the click of the TV followed by the sounds of the Mets game. I could tell by Michael's moans and groans that they were losing.

I stood barefoot in the kitchen, enjoying the cool, green ceramic tile floor, and opened the freezer door. I was so hot, I contemplated climbing in, but there was no room for my big belly. *Oh, well. There's Häagen Dazs Chocolate Peanut Butter, my favorite.* Just as I removed the lid from the pint carton, a gush of fluid and water exploded from my body.

"Ahhhh!" I screamed. "What the fuck?" I dumped the ice cream on the counter. "Michael!" *Shit, I really want that ice cream!* I ran into the den. "My water broke!"

"Are you sure?" he asked, still looking at the TV.

"What the hell do you think this is?" I tugged at my wet clothes as another burst came shooting out of me, right in front of him.

"Oh, my God!" I had Michael's attention now. He jumped up and started running around the room, not knowing where to go or what to do first.

"Calm down, Michael. This doesn't mean I'm going into labor, it just means my water broke." He started up the stairs, three at a time.

"I'll get your bag," he yelled down to me.

We were so unprepared for this moment. I had a C-section scheduled in two weeks. This was not supposed to happen. Dr. Tebbe was in Florida and was going to fly in to assist in my delivery. I doubted she would make it at this point.

I was surprisingly calm as I walked up the stairs to get changed. Michael was frantically throwing clothes into my overnight bag.

"Honey, relax. It's fine. We just have to be calm." No sooner than the words came out of my mouth, I screamed in pain.

"Oh, shit!" My first contraction felt like someone grabbed hold of my insides and squeezed with a superhero's grip. It was my turn to panic. "Let's go! Hurry up!"

"Sylvia, it's okay, it's okay. Here, sit down and breathe or

something. Isn't that what you're supposed to do? Breathe?"
He cleared off a space for me on the edge of the bed and I sat
down, the blood rushing to my head.

"How the hell should I know?" I yelled at him. Since
we weren't planning for natural childbirth, I had decided to
forego Lamaze classes. I was under the impression that with
a C-section, they just wheeled you in and took out the baby.
I was so not ready for this.

I took deep breaths and tried to stay calm. There was no
time for me to change. Looking into my eyes, Michael smiled
a sweet, soothing smile and, for a moment, my panic sub-
sided. Then another contraction grabbed hold of my lower
body and squeezed like a vice. I fell back onto the bed.

"Ahhhh!" I exhaled a scream.

"Breathe, honey. Just breathe." Michael tried to ease my
anxiety, but I was having none of it.

"You fucking breathe!" I screamed at him. He had some
nerve. *It's his fault I am dying here and he tells me to breathe.*

"Come on, let's go." He pulled me to my feet, grabbed my
bag and scurried down the stairs. I waddled after him as fast
as I could. He was in the car with the motor running before
I reached the porch. I waddled like a penguin to the passenger side of the car. Michael jumped out and opened the door
for me, helping me settle into the seat.

The tires squealed against the pavement as Michael threw
the car into reverse and whipped out of the driveway. The
hospital was normally a 30-minute drive from our house and
Michael was doing his best to shorten that. I closed my eyes
and tried to stay calm. The contractions continued and sweat
poured from my body. My body was stuck to my clothes and
my clothes were stuck to the seat.

We weaved in and out of traffic; Michael was driving like a maniac. I peeked over to the dashboard and saw the speedometer — 110 mph.

"Michael, you're going to get us killed — or pulled over!" I yelled.

It was as if I summoned the police with mind. No sooner than the words were out of my mouth, the car filled with red and blue light and the piercing wail of a siren. Michael pulled the car over to the shoulder of the road and we waited while a New Jersey state trooper loped up to the car door and tapped on the window.

I was still heaving and panting from my last contraction and was a puddle in the passenger seat. The officer looked in and I tried to smile. He immediately understood the situation.

"My wife is in labor," Michael blurted. "We're trying to get to the . . ."

"Go! Just go," the officer insisted. "I'll call in your plates. No one will stop you. Now get out of here. And be careful. And congratulations." We were already pulling away, waving, as the officer patted the trunk of the car, like a cowboy sending a horse on its way.

For the rest of the ride, I held on tight. I called Marianna to let her know what was happening, but I thought better of calling my mother. With things going so far off the plan, I knew she would be a worried wreck. Michael pulled up at the hospital entrance and lurched the car into park. He jumped out, ran around to the driver's side and, before I really knew what was happening, I was being whisked into the admissions area. In the blur, I heard Michael and the admissions clerk arguing about an insurance card, and then time stopped.

I was 5 centimeters dilated when we arrived and they seemed to be in no hurry to get me admitted.

Marianna and Chip arrived at the hospital and Michael had someone call my doctor in Florida to tell her what was happening. I was so unprepared and fearful, but Dr. Tebbe spoke with me on the phone and calmed me down.

"Sylvia, just relax. I know you're scared, but everything is going to be fine."

"But this isn't how it was supposed to go. I need you here."

"I know. But the baby comes when the baby's ready. Dr. Weiss will take good care of you, I promise."

"Okay."

"Okay. You can do this. Good luck, honey. I'm rooting for you."

"Thanks." I managed a little smile.

Finally, after what seemed like hours, I was taken to the maternity ward. I felt like I was in a movie about childbirth — the cursing, the screaming, the demands for drugs and my husband's penis on a platter — it was all happening. Mostly, I wanted drugs. When the orderly and I arrived at the delivery room, a waiting nurse stripped off my wet clothes and put me in a gown. I didn't put up a fight until she went for my shoes.

"No, leave them," I insisted.

"Ms. Lasalandra, you don't need your shoes in surgery," she reassured me.

"I don't go anywhere without my shoes. I'm too short without them." I could not be convinced. I kicked my feet to keep her from taking them.

"Ma'am, please. You'll be lying down." Her tone changed from gently persuading to commanding. "You cannot wear your shoes into surgery." She gave a look to the orderly, who held my legs down while she removed my platform sneakers. I was furious, but in no position to fight them.

My labor lasted for about an hour before I went into delivery. Marianna and Chip stayed with me until they wheeled me into the operating room. Michael held my hand as Dr. Weiss and the assisting physician, Dr. Hurt, finally gave the okay. It was time.

I was given a spinal epidural and, within 20 seconds, I was numb from the shoulders down. I was really getting impatient and worried about the delivery, but I couldn't keep my mind focused on what was happening. The doctors began asking me questions as they prepped me.

"How's the restaurant doing?" Dr. Weiss inquired.

"Great. Really great." I was taken aback. I thought he would ask how *I* was doing.

"When's the new one going to open?" Dr. Hurt joined the conversation.

"Soon." *What is going on here?*

"We're having a cookout next weekend," Dr. Hurt said. "What kind of wine do you recommend with tuna steaks?"

"Um . . . Pinot Grigio." *This is unbelievable.*

"You know, Sylvia, the wife and I were in a couple of weeks ago and, wow, that was great polenta."

"Just cut me open and get this over with," I yelled with exasperation.

"Sorry," Dr. Weiss laughed. "We are just about ready."

I closed my eyes and the doctors began the procedure. The smell of burning flesh from the laser incision filled the room. My throat tightened and I stifled a cough. All of a sudden, I felt the pressure of the baby being pulled from my uterus. It felt like my insides were being ripped out.

"What are you doing?" I demanded.

"Everything is fine, Ms. Lasalandra. The baby is almost out," Dr. Hurt informed me.

"Honey, you're doing great," Michael encouraged me, wiping my brow. I was so tired. I just wanted to sleep, to close my eyes and wake to find my life back the way it was.

"Oh, my God!" Michael gasped. "There she is. Syl, she's here. You did it!"

I couldn't see beyond the tent they erected to keep me from watching myself being cut open, and there was no noise in the delivery room. I started to panic.

"Why don't I hear my baby? I don't hear my baby!" I screamed. She was out. She was supposed to be screaming, too.

"It's okay, Sylvia," Dr. Weiss chimed in. "We're just cleaning her esophagus." And with that, a wail let loose that was terrifying, joyful music to my ears. *Oh, my God. I have a baby. I am a mother.*

"Okay, baby, I hear you," I told her in an exhausted whisper, but she continued to scream. She was passed around from nurse to nurse, each one checking and inspecting her. The head pediatrician came in and took her footprints. Once she was clean and dry and scrubbed and polished, they wrapped her in a blue blanket and handed her to Michael.

"Here's your new daughter, Mr. Frodella. Five pounds, twelve ounces of perfect baby girl," the nurse said, beaming. Tears welled up in Michael's eyes. He looked so happy.

She continued to cry as he gently bounced and cooed for her, and then he held her down where I could see her. Her mouth was wide open and the shrieks were unmistakably from my daughter. I looked at her for the first time. She was so tiny and perfect; I could barely believe she was real.

45

"It's okay, Melina, Mommy's here," I whispered to my perfect, beautiful daughter. The crying stopped instantly. She barely turned her tiny head toward me and dropped immediately to sleep.

"Can you believe that?" one of the nurses said to Dr. Weiss. They all shook their heads in wonder. My own head fell back to the pillow and I passed out from exhaustion.

I awoke a few minutes later to the screams and wails of a woman in the throes of natural childbirth. Groggy from the sedatives and anesthesia, I was disoriented and confused. The recovery room was fuzzy and strange.

"I don't want to do that... I don't want to do that!" I shouted at the nurse.

"You've had your baby," the nurse reassured me.

"I don't want to do that!"

"You've already had your baby, Ms. Lasalandra," she repeated.

"Oh," I sighed, and fell back to sleep.

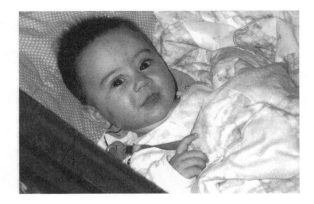

Melina in her bassinette

Five

This Is the Happiest Time of My Life?

I remember leaving the hospital thinking, "Wait, are they going to let me just walk off with him? I don't know beans about babies! I don't have a license to do this!"

—Anne Tyler, novelist

The next day, I awoke with excruciating pain in my abdomen and overwhelming nausea. I could only lie on my side and I could barely lift my head from the pillow. I had been moved to a private suite and it took a moment before my eyes became adjusted to the half-light in the room. The nurse on duty poked her head in to check on me. She smiled sweetly and came in.

"Good morning," she chirped, opening the mauve curtains. "How do you feel today?"

"Like shit," I murmured, squinting as the sunlight took over the room.

"You'll get your strength back soon. Don't you worry."

She came around and checked my IV. "Would you like to see your baby? I can bring her in for you."

What? I thought to myself. *Is she crazy?*

"Do you really think I want to see my baby?" I snapped at her. She looked surprised, but didn't change her annoyingly cheerful tone.

"Well, if you're not feeling up to it now, that's okay. Your brother is here to see you."

"Great." I was not in the mood for visitors, but I was aware of the inevitability. I couldn't put them off for long. *May as well get it over with*, I thought. My brother John burst into the room like a jack-in-the-box.

"Good morning, Mommy," he sing-songed. His enthusiasm and energy was pissing me off. I wanted to tell him to fuck off, but I bit my tongue. "Syl, you are a mom! I can't believe it. Where's the baby?"

"I don't know. Where's yours?" My head was still fuzzy from sleep and painkillers.

"Lara's with Joe. They'll drop by later. Now, let's see this kid. I'll get the nurse to bring her in."

"It's okay, you don't have to."

"But I want to see her." John jumped up and down like a little kid, clapping his hands. I stifled a laugh, hiding my face so he couldn't see me. John left the room to follow his quest. I tried to focus on the flowers that surrounded me: so many beautiful bouquets from so many friends. John's was the biggest by far. "Showy queen," I thought with a smirk.

John returned with a nurse and a smile.

"So, Ms. Lasalandra, are you ready to see your baby now?"

"Not really," I groaned. "But I guess that doesn't matter." I could barely lift my head. How was I supposed to hold my baby?

"I'll be right back," the nurse said.

"Syl, how do you feel?" John asked, noticing for the first time that I wasn't myself.

"Like shit. How do you think I feel?" I snapped. Less than I wanted his enthusiasm did I want his sympathy.

"Well," his voice dripping with sarcasm, "you look great."

I wanted to punch him.

"Kiss my ass." I closed my eyes, turning my face away from him, but smiled in spite of myself. John smirked and sat on the edge of my bed.

"Here she is," the nurse proclaimed, entering with Melina tightly wrapped in a blue blanket. I thought my heart might explode, and not in a good way. Anxiety was gripping me and I lay there frozen with terror. She was right there, tiny and helpless. I wanted to scream at the nurse, "Get her out of the room. I don't want her!" *Maybe John would want her. Maybe the nurse would want her.*

"Go ahead, John, you can hold her." It was last thing I wanted to do. *She is so small. What am I supposed to do with her?*

"Oh, Syl, she's beautiful. She's just beautiful," John cooed, taking Melina from the nurse.

Yeah, beautiful, I thought, *but terrifying just the same. How can I ever love something that scares me so much?*

The rest of the day went much the same way — friends and family, in and out. Luckily, everyone wanted to hold Melina, so I didn't have to. I was so nauseated from the painkillers, I ate nothing all day. Late in the evening, after all the visitors had come and gone, the nurse peeked into my room.

"Marianna is here to stay with you, Ms. Lasalandra. Shall I bring in Melina so you can feed her?"

"No. I can barely feed myself."

"All right, Ms. Lasalandra, it's okay. I'll bring her in tomorrow morning. Now you get some rest." The nurse backed out of the room and held the door open for Marianna.

"Hi, Syl, honey." The concern in her voice nearly broke my heart. "You look so tired. How do you feel?"

"Terrible." Tears started welling up in my eyes. All the pain and fear I had been bottling up all day gushed out in a torrent of tears. "I don't understand. I'm supposed to be happy, but I'm not. I'm miserable. I don't know what's happening." Tears poured down my face and my chest heaved under the weight of my sobs. "This is supposed to be the best day of my life, and I just want to die."

"It's okay, honey, let it out. It's okay." Marianna sat on the edge of the bed and put her arms around me. "You are going to be feeling a lot of conflicting emotions. Your hormones are out of control and your life is turning upside down. You are allowed to be scared and uncertain. Just don't hold it in."

She rocked me and stroked my hair while I cried, repeating, "It's okay. It's okay." Although I took momentary solace in her comforting embrace, I knew in my heart that it wasn't okay. I had no hope things were ever going to be the same again.

The following morning, the nurse came in bright and early to wake me. Marianna was folding up the green and pink floral pullout couch next to my bed. She stayed with me every night while I was in the hospital.

"Good morning," Marianna greeted the nurse.

"Good morning. Ms. Lasalandra, would you like me to bring in Melina? You could feed her, if you're feeling up to it."

I was feeling better, but I didn't want to be anywhere near the baby. I wanted to rest. I wanted to forget. *I only have a few days of hospital time to recover and they keep forcing the kid on me like there aren't a million people here to take care of her.* I could barely control the resentment and terror building up inside.

"No, I still feel really nauseated," I lied. Although I still felt terrible, the nausea was gone for the most part, but I wasn't feeling any bond with the baby. I didn't want to hold her, to feed her, to change her. I didn't even want to look at her. My guilt and shame rivaled the pain in my abdomen. I didn't want this baby, but here she was. I could barely admit this to myself, let alone anyone else.

"Oh, well, okay," the nurse snipped. "When do you think you will want to start feeding and changing her?"

"In about fifteen years," I replied sarcastically. Marianna laughed, but the look on her face betrayed her concern.

"Syl, I've got to run." Marianna patted my shoulder and kissed my forehead. "Call me if you need anything and I'll be back tonight."

"Okay, great," I replied, relieved to be left alone. Marianna and the nurse left the room and I braced myself for the onslaught of visitors.

My mother, father and Aunt Lina had just left for lunch when the burning sensation in my breasts became unbearable. All morning they felt oddly warm, but I had shrugged it off and tried to concentrate on my family and friends. So many people came to see Melina and me. Luckily, everyone wanted to hold her, so I still didn't have to. Once I was alone, the pain and burning took center stage.

I peeked under my gown and could not believe my eyes. My breasts looked like two huge, red watermelons! I had gone from a C to an EE overnight. When my gown covered me, I looked like I had one big tit instead of two. *What is happening to my body? What has she done to me?* I felt like I was on fire. I buzzed for the nurse, and pounced the moment she walked in.

"What happened to my tits?" I screamed, lifting my gown for her to see. "They are five times bigger than they were yesterday, and they're hot as shit!"

"Ms. Lasalandra, your breasts are engorged. That means your milk is coming in."

"What?"

"Didn't anyone tell you about this? Didn't you read any books about birthing?"

"No." I felt scolded and ashamed. *There had been no time. Didn't anyone understand?*

"Well, you have two options. If you are planning to breast feed, we can pump your milk and that will relieve some of the pressure. If you don't want to breast feed, we'll put some cold compresses on you to alleviate some of your discomfort until you stop producing milk. Have you made any decisions about feeding?"

"Yes." Before Melina was born, we had decided I would not breast feed. "I gave her life, I'm not giving her my breast milk."

"Very well," the nurse sniffed. "I'll bring you some ice."

No matter what I did, I felt I was being judged. After only two days, I was already a horrible mother, and everyone knew it. I wanted to scream and cry and wail and thrash about. My body was no longer my own and neither was my mind. "This is supposed to be the happiest time of my life!" I wanted to yell from the rooftops. *Where is the instant bonding I was promised?* Every time they brought Melina into the room, I wanted to crawl into the corner and curl into a ball, but there was no place to hide. *Does Melina know? If I look into her eyes, she will know. She can see inside me and see the hatred and fear. She will know that I want her to be gone, to go back where she came from.*

My desperation was growing by the minute and relief seemed impossible. The more the people around me focused their attention my way, the more I wanted to run. *It won't be long*, I thought. *It won't be long before everyone knows my secret; I am a bad mother and a terrible person.*

Marianna came out of the bathroom, gave me a little wave and walked out the door into the hallway. As I watched her leave, tears welled up in my eyes. I was so envious of her; I wanted nothing more than to get up from my bed and go to the bathroom on my own. I was sick of the catheter and sponge baths; tired of depending on the nursing staff for every little thing.

On Saturday, when I'd had my bath, I tried to make jokes with the young woman assigned to my hygiene needs, but she was unresponsive. Word was already out that I was trouble, that I didn't want my baby, that I was a "handful." *Do they think I am some kind of princess who doesn't want to get her hands dirty? They don't know me*, I thought. *I work hard...I can do for myself...Can't I just change my mind about this motherhood thing?*

Marianna returned a few moments later with a nurse I'd never seen before. She smiled and came to my side.

"Good morning, Ms. Lasalandra. Let's get this catheter out and let you get up a little." She was giving me back some of my freedom, and I wanted to kiss her.

"I'll help her go to the bathroom," Marianna offered.

"Is that okay, Ms. Lasalandra?" the nurse asked sweetly. I nodded gratefully.

Slowly, I sat up and the nurse helped me swing my legs over the side of the bed. I felt so weak and sore; a dull ache permeated my body. The stitches in my abdomen would take weeks to heal, but I feared my soul would never recover. The joy of motherhood was supposed to alleviate the physical pain, or so I believed, but I had no joy, no elation, no relief in my heart. I felt cheated and deceived.

"Come on, sweetie. It'll feel good to go to the bathroom on your own," Marianna said as she took my hands and gently pulled me to my feet.

I mumbled an affirmation and let her slowly, carefully guide me to the bathroom. My limbs felt useless and rubbery. My belly and breasts throbbed and pulsed. Marianna helped me situate myself gingerly in the chair-equipped hospital toilet and turned her back to give me a bit of privacy.

The door to the room opened and the nurse came back in, this time carrying Melina. *Can't I even pee in peace?*

"Time for her morning feeding," the nurse called out. All the anxiety and fear came flooding back over me. I searched for any excuse to delay this moment.

"Now? I'm still feeling pretty nauseous," I shouted from

the bathroom. "And I'm really sore. I don't think I can hold her."

"Don't be silly." The nurse was unfazed. "She only weighs five pounds. Of course you can hold her." She waited until I emerged and then plopped the little bundle of blue blanket into my arms. I wanted to drop her like a hot potato. I wanted someone to catch her, of course, but I did not want to be the one holding her.

The nurse handed me a bottle of formula and waited while I adjusted myself and put the bottle to Melina's tiny lips. Through half-closed eyes I looked down at her, afraid of what I would see. She was sweet and quiet — she had rarely cried in her first two days of life — and she looked up at me as if she knew I was her mother. She took the bottle eagerly, staring at me. I looked away; I couldn't meet her gaze. Marianna sat on the edge of the bed and watched me. *What did she see?* I wondered. *Was I fooling her? Did she think I was enjoying this? Did she think the instincts of motherhood had suddenly taken hold?*

"Syl, I know this is hard, honey," Marianna whispered. She knew the truth. I wasn't fooling her.

"I'm fine," I lied. "Do you want a turn?"

"You are doing great. I'll take her in a little while."

"Oh, look! There she is!" my mother gushed, bursting through the door, my father right behind her. Ma stopped and clasped her hands to her cheeks. "They are so beautiful!"

"Hi, Ma. Hi, Papá." I was genuinely glad to see them. "Ma, you want to take Melina?"

"Of course," Ma said enthusiastically, taking Melina from my arms and settling into the overstuffed armchair across from my bed. She whispered and cooed at Melina, finishing the chore I couldn't. Marianna patted me on the leg, stood from my bedside and grabbed her purse from the end table next to the couch.

"Syl, I'm going to go. I'll be back later for another slumber party." I tried to smile, but I was unsuccessful. "Good to see you, Carmella. Bye, John."

"Bye-bye, Marianna." My mother held her cheek out to be kissed. Papá nodded and gave Marianna a little wave as she closed the door behind her. Then he looked at me with kind, understanding eyes.

"Are you feeling better today, Sylvia?" he asked, taking a seat on the pullout couch.

"Yeah, a little. I went to the bathroom by myself."

"Good for you, honey," Ma smiled. "Nicky and Kim are coming today; they should be here soon."

"Great," I deadpanned. I wanted no more visitors. I wanted to be home in my bed with the covers over my head. We sat in silence for what seemed a lifetime. Ma finished feeding Melina and rocked her gently to sleep. It didn't look so difficult, but it terrified me. I was in the grip of a senseless fear. I wanted to say something to my mother, to let her know that something was wrong, but I didn't know how to bring it up. I had never needed her help before: at least not like this.

Suddenly, the room was filled with people. My confession would have to wait. My brother, Nicky, arrived with his wife, Kim, and their three children, Giovanni, Marilyn and Martino. Melina was passed around from grownup to grownup and shown to the kids.

"Look, Martino," Kim said to her one-month-old son, whom she held in her arms. "This is your cousin Melina. You are going to have so much fun playing together when you get bigger." Giovanni and Marilyn peered into the bundle Nicky was holding.

"Ziza, is this your baby?" Marilyn asked me.

"Yep, that's Melina."

"She's so little," Giovanni observed.

"She's only three days old." *Too little to exist*, I thought. *Too little for me to handle.* I loved being an aunt. Giovanni and Marilyn were terrific kids — eight and six. I could handle eight and six. You could talk to them and play with them — and give them back to their parents when you were done.

"Nicky," I asked, "you want to trade Giovanni or Marilyn for Melina? We could trade back when she's fifteen or so."

"Yeah, right," he laughed. "That's a fair trade." If he only knew I wasn't kidding. I would have traded in a second. The nurse came in to take Melina back to the nursery.

"No. Let her stay," I protested, playing the big shot. "My family wants to see her." As long as there were people around to hold her and watch her, I didn't mind Melina's presence.

Michael and more of the family arrived and settled in for the day. My mother sat protectively by my side and held my hand. Michael beamed and Aunt Lina cooed. I kept up as brave a face as I could, loudly demanding, "Isn't she cute?" and "Can you believe she's so gorgeous?" On the outside everything looked normal, but I am a terrible liar and wear my heart on my sleeve. I knew I could not keep the pretense up much longer. Inside my head was a maze of confusion, and I was trapped. No matter which turn I took, I came to a dead end.

. . .

Once everyone was gone, I snuck in a shower. I felt so dirty and disgusting from lying in bed, and from the sick, terrifying thoughts in my head. Slowly, I hoisted myself out of bed, shuffled to the bathroom and turned the faucet. Just the sound of gushing water against the white fiberglass was enough to fill me with anticipation. Finally, something familiar, something I knew.

As the cool water washed over my hot, tired body, I felt a relief, as if all the agonies of the past few days were floating away in rivulets on my olive skin, into the tub and down the drain. Who could believe a shower could so elevate my spirit? I felt I could face the world again.

Scrubbed and clean and wearing a fresh gown, I called the nurse to change my sheets. I waited on the pullout couch until I could return to my bed. Newly washed linens replaced the sweaty, damp ones I had wallowed in for two days. I closed my eyes and took a deep breath, taking in the smell of clean and relishing the soft cotton against my cool skin. *Maybe I can get a little sleep. Maybe things aren't so bad after all.*

Marianna came back that evening, as she did every night. I was feeling so much better since my shower and I think I even smiled when Marianna returned.

"You look better," Marianna said encouragingly. "What have you been up to?"

"I snuck a shower while no one was looking."

"Good for you. You want to go for a walk? Let's go over to the nursery and see the baby," she said.

"Okay. If we have to." She helped me out of bed, on with my robe and took my elbow, gently guiding me down the hall.

Nurses and doctors scurried about, busy at their tasks. I envied them their freedom to come and go as they pleased, their purpose and direction. I envied Michael, too. Together we made this baby, and I was the one left to deal with it. Of course, Michael had his hands full running the restaurant without me, but I would have traded places in a minute. I wanted out of this prison of pain and fear. When he did visit, he filled me in about the restaurant, the staff, how the work was coming along on the new place. He missed me and I missed him. We had always shared everything, and I suddenly felt isolated from him, like we were strangers meeting in uncertain times.

Marianna and I reached the nursery's picture window and peered in at all the babies. The cribs were in neat rows and each baby was wrapped snuggly in a hospital-issued blanket and cap with just a little face peeking through. They were all sleeping peacefully, except for one. Melina was wailing at the top of her lungs. It was the first time I had heard her cry since the day she was born. My heart pounded and a panic I had never experienced overtook me.

"Why is she crying? Why aren't they picking her up?"

"I'm sure she's fine, honey. Babies cry," Marianna said, trying to calm me.

"She's not fine. She's screaming!" I banged my fist on the glass. "Why is my baby crying? What is going on in there?"

A nurse I recognized came to the window. A glimmer of hope surged in me. I had instincts after all.

"Hi, Ms. Lasalandra," she said, smiling.

"Why is my baby crying?" I yelled again through the glass.

"Oh, we haven't had a chance to feed her yet," she explained, like nothing was wrong.

"Well, then, feed her!" *What was wrong with them? Why didn't they just feed her?*

"We will. It'll just be another minute or so before her

bottle is ready." She was very professional and kept an even tone.

"Well, at least pick her up!" I was outraged. "We are paying you to take care of our baby and there she is, screaming in hunger!"

"Syl, calm down," Marianna said, patting my hand. "They're going to feed her. She's not going to starve."

I just stared at them.

"Come on, sweetie. You're tired. Let's go back to your room." Marianna guided me away from the window, looking back at the nurse apologetically. I felt like two people trapped in one body. She knew something was wrong.

Everyone who knew me and loved me sensed something had changed. Marianna was a mental health professional, and the red flags were flying at the top of the rafters for her. My mother had her own experiences to draw from and saw in me a pattern she knew all too well. No one dared utter the words postpartum depression — not yet. Even though they knew the truth, no one wanted to believe it.

Late in the afternoon on the day before my discharge from the hospital, my best friend, Kelly, arrived with two adorable outfits for Melina. I was so happy to see her; she was always like a ray of sunshine — calm, smiling and warm.

"Syl, how are you?" She had been in the visitation loop and sensed my discomfort.

"I've been better."

"Well, I'm here to cheer you up. Look at these," she chimed, pulling from her shopping bag a sweet little pink dress and a tiny onesie with monkeys and matching hat. "I thought these were just precious."

"They really are, Kel." I started to tear up.

"Syl, it's okay." Kelly patted my hand as she sat on the bed next to me. "The blues will pass. Your hormones are all out of whack for the first couple of days after the birth and it really does a number on your head. It happens to everybody."

Although I was sure what I was feeling was more than the "baby blues," I wanted to believe in Kelly's optimism. I took a deep breath and pulled myself together. The door opened a crack and a nurse poked his head through.

"Time for baby's first picture," he announced, brining in Melina uninvited and thrusting her into my arms.

"So much for girl talk," I groused.

"Well, she's a girl," the nurse keenly observed. Kelly bit her tongue to keep from laughing.

"But you're not," I snarled. He cut me a look and called back over his shoulder.

"Everybody's decent," he said, opening the door for the photographer. Kelly, in true best friend fashion, sensed my anxiety and immediately took over the situation.

"Let's see," she directed. "Let's open this window and get some natural light in here. No one looks good under fluorescents."

The hospital photographer agreed as he set up his camera. Kelly helped him pose the baby and, while making further lighting and angle suggestions, cooed and giggled for Melina.

"What do you think about this, Syl?" Kelly asked, holding Melina's little hand behind her head like a supermodel.

"Nice," I laughed. "Maybe we could get her a swimsuit."

"Now, that's the spirit." Kelly giggled.

I was amazed and grateful for Kelly's organization and supervision, and I swelled a little watching everyone fuss over my little girl. Underneath, though, my agitation still bubbled. *I don't even want this baby. Why would I want a picture of her?*

"Perfection!" the photographer finally conceded. "You have a lovely baby, Ms. Lasalandra. It's been a pleasure. I'll now remove myself from your hair."

"Thank you," I said as sincerely as I could. "Ciao."

"Now that wasn't so bad, was it?" Kelly said to Melina, picking her up from the little bassinette.

"I guess not," I sighed.

"I wasn't talking to you," Kelly teased. The nurse came back in.

"Would you like me to take Melina, Ms. Lasalandra, or would you like to feed her? It's that time."

"You can take her," I said, more eagerly than I intended. I wanted to play it cool in front of Kelly, but my resistance was wearing down.

"It's going to be okay, Syl. You're exhausted and out of sorts. It's going to be fine." Kelly tried to reassure me, but I panicked at the thought of taking her home without nurses to whisk her away.

I lay awake that night, tossing and turning, unable to get comfortable. Marianna kept asking if I needed anything, but I could think of nothing — nothing I could say out loud. What I really needed was someone to take the baby.

Six

Is Anybody Listening?

Postpartum depression can strike within the first few days after the birth of a child and any time within the first two years.

M s. Lasalandra," the nurse said unfazed, "that's crazy. You don't really want me to take your baby."

"Yes, I do. You are really good with her and I don't want her. She's yours. I'm sure it'll be better that way."

"Lots of women get the baby blues. Giving birth is hard on the body and the mind, and it can make you have strange thoughts. But it'll pass. Just give yourself a little time."

"But I don't have any time. They are sending me home today. Maybe I could just stay here a little longer."

"I don't think so. Once you're home and can settle into a routine, you'll see that everything is going to be fine."

"Maybe I could go home and Melina could stay here for a few more weeks. That way, she'll be bigger and I'll be able to handle her better."

"Ms. Lasalandra, you can't leave your baby in the hospital.

She's perfectly healthy and belongs with you. It's time for you to take her home and start taking care of her."

"But, I can't"

"Yes, you can. The baby blues will pass and you'll be feeling great in a couple of weeks."

"But, what if I don't?"

"You will."

We were both getting exasperated.

"But what if I don't?"

"You will." She stood to return my discharge papers to the nurse's station. "Now get yourself together. Your husband will be here shortly to take you home." I knew what I was feeling would not just pass. I had to make her hear me.

"What if I give her up for adoption — or take her to a police station?" I'd heard on the news that in the state of New Jersey, there is a law that allows a person to leave a child at a police station with no questions asked, to prevent desperate mothers from abandoning their babies on the streets.

"Ms. Lasalandra, now listen to me. I know it's scary having a baby, but your maternal instincts will kick in any day now and you'll know what to do. You'll feed her and change her and love her. Just relax, go home and care for your daughter. She needs you." She paused at the door and turned back to look at me. Without making eye contact, she repeated the phrase I'd come to loathe: "Everything will be fine."

I lay back onto the bed. I was dressed in my own clothes, ready to go home. My parents were at my house awaiting our arrival. I wanted to run. Maybe adoption was a good idea. I knew I couldn't take her to the police station. Too many people knew me in our town. The word would be around in no time that crazy Sylvia left her kid with the cops. Adoption was the only other answer.

Wait! Michael is so forgetful, maybe he forgot the car seat. That's it. New Jersey state law says that a hospital cannot release an infant without a car seat. If Michael didn't bring it, then she would have to stay here. I could go home and figure out what to do.

My spirits lifted and I started to feel excited about going home. Melina would stay at the hospital, where people could take care of her, and I could get on with my life. I thanked God for making Michael so scatterbrained and prayed that today would be no different from any other day. The nurse brought in Melina and put her in my arms.

"Aren't you going to carry her down?" I asked.

"No. I have to stay here. Your husband can take your bags and you can take Melina." She paused and patted my shoulder. "You'll be fine."

You'll be fine, you'll be fine. That's all anyone ever says around here. What does she know? What does anybody know? I wanted to shoot someone, mostly myself.

Michael came into the room, followed by an orderly with a wheelchair.

"Hi, beautiful," he said, kissing the top of my head. "Hi, little one," he whispered to Melina. "Are you ready to go?"

"Yeah, I guess," I said. "Did you remember the car seat, Michael?' I held my breath. *Say no. Say no,* I chanted under my breath.

"Of course, I did. It's right here," he laughed, reaching just outside the doorway and producing the offending safety device. "I'm not that forgetful."

My heart dropped to my stomach. *He can never remember where he leaves his keys. He loses the remote all the time. How did he remember to bring the car seat?*

"Good," I said, trying to hold back the tears.

I didn't have much time. I was being wheeled out into the world. I needed a plan. I made a mental list of the people we passed, considering the suitability of each to become my daughter's new parent. No one here on the maternity ward. They already had children. They wouldn't appreciate her. I needed to find someone who really wanted a kid. And it had to be someone in the hospital. An adoption agency would take time, too much time. She was going home with me now.

The orderly pushed the button on the elevator and we started our descent. I would be free very soon. My heart raced. I glanced down at Melina, sleeping in my arms. She would be fine here. This could work.

"She's a beautiful baby, ma'am," the orderly said, breaking the silence. "As beautiful as her mother." If he knew what I was planning to do, he would never have said I was beautiful.

"Thank you," I murmured.

The elevator came to a soft landing on the first floor and the silvery doors parted. We emerged into a lobby filled with people, continued on through the sliding doors of the hospital, out into the gray, hazy day and down the sidewalk. A young black couple approached us. The woman looked like she was due to give birth any minute. She looked at me holding Melina in my arms and gave me a little smile.

"So," she asked hesitantly, "how was it?" It took all my strength not to yell out to her, "Turn back now! This is your last chance!"

"It was fine," I said, biting my tongue. "You'll be fine." I repeated the mantra I had learned on the inside.

"Thanks," the man said. "She's pretty nervous. But it looks like things turned out well for you. That's a beautiful . . . ," he trailed off, momentarily embarrassed.

"Girl." I finished his compliment and smiled weakly. "Thank you. Good luck in there." As they went on their way, I muttered under my breath, "You could have this one, too. Buy one, get one free."

Reaching the car, Michael put my bags in the trunk and fastened the ugly brown car seat into the back. I cringed as it mocked me.

"Thank you, sir," Michael said politely to the orderly. "I'll take over from here."

"Yes, sir." The orderly smiled and helped me of the chair. "Now you take good care of those beautiful ladies."

"I will," Michael said, shaking his hand. He took Melina and fastened her in. She was so small, too small. The car seat swallowed her up. I worried it wouldn't hold her in, not the way Michael drove. Then Michael helped me into the front seat and buckled my seat belt.

I was silent for the entire ride home, cocooned in my guilt and shame. I never once looked back to see if Melina was okay. *What kind of horrible monster doesn't want its own baby? What kind of woman has no empathy, no impulse to protect her offspring? Who have I become?*

The welcoming committee was waiting on the lawn in front of our shuttered Cape Cod-style house as Michael pulled the car into the driveway. A huge, pink-lettered "It's a Girl" sign was staked in the front yard. My mother stood on the cobblestone walk snapping pictures, while my father captured it all on video. I took a deep breath to fortify myself. I didn't know how much more I could take.

We got out of the car and Michael handed Melina to me.

Can't he take her in? I'd rather carry the bags. But I did not protest. The attention was already more than I bargained for. Ma continued taking photos as we strolled up the walk and into the house. I couldn't believe my eyes when I opened the front door. An enormous hot air balloon basket, overflowing with gifts from our friends Karen and Dave was among the plenteous flowers and dazzlingly wrapped packages that filled the living room. Gifts were stacked on the wrought iron wine cages and draped on the chaise. My "wine haven for a wine maven" looked like a baby store had exploded in it. Aunt Lina, my father's sister, in her housecoat as always, beamed by the dining room table, cascading with even more presents. All this fuss was for me — and the baby I didn't want. I didn't deserve it. *If my ass wasn't so big*, I thought, *I could just crawl in that basket and fly away*. I did the next best thing. With uncontrollable tears welling up in my eyes, I handed Ma the baby and ran up the stairs to my room. Like a crushed teenager, I slammed the door and collapsed on the bed in a torrent of sobs.

Seven

Home Scary Home

Tonight I see how scared I am. There is so much to do for
this little creature who screams and wiggles.

—David Steinberg, comedian and writer

I stood on the front porch, holding Melina under my arm
like a football, screaming at Michael. It was my first full
day home from the hospital, and I snapped.

"Nothing has changed for you! You can come and go as
you please and I am stuck here!"

"Sylvia, I have to go to work," he pleaded, one foot in the
car and one on the driveway.

"Go. Just go!"

"Sylvia, what can I do to help you?"

"I can't figure out the baby formula." I collapsed on the
porch with Melina in my lap. "It has to be measured just right
or she'll get too much, and there are all those bottles and
nipples... I can't do it. I just can't do it." Tears streamed
down my face.

"Honey, I'll be right back, okay? I'm just going to go to
the corner store. I'll be right back."

"Fine. Whatever." I sank down onto the porch and the sobs continued until Michael returned. Melina lay in my lap like a rag doll. It was all I could do to be that close to her. My mother was on her way over to help out and Aunt Lina was in the kitchen cooking for our little army, trying to understand what was happening to me. I had plenty of people around to help me, but I wanted my husband. I knew he had to work, that our restaurant was not going to run itself, but I was so overwhelmed by all the recent changes in my life, I couldn't bear the thought of him going about his usual business without me.

A few minutes later, Michael came back, just as he promised, carrying several bags from Stop & Shop.

"Honey, I got you some things that'll make your life a little easier. Come in the house, okay?" He coaxed me up from the brick front steps and I followed him inside. He spread out three six-packs of single-serve prepared infant formula on the kitchen counter, a package of nipples that fit the formula and some ginger ale for me.

"Now, look. You just shake it up, take off the cap, peel back the foil, put the nipple on and it's ready to go. Infant fast food!" I was so touched by his gesture that I burst into tears.

"Honey, I'm sorry. I was just trying to help." I buried my face in his chest and he wrapped his long arms around me. I was still holding Melina.

"No, it's great. Thank you. Really. Thank you." My words were directed into his shirt, but he got the idea.

"Okay. I'm going to go to work now. Are you going to be okay?"

"I'm fine. Aunt Lina's here and Ma's on her way,"

"Okay. Call me if you need anything. I'll see you tonight."

He kissed Melina's fuzzy, little head and kissed me goodbye. "I love you."

"Bye. I love you, too." *Now where did Aunt Lina go, and why am I still holding this kid?*

My first few days home from the hospital were a blur of tears, unwanted presents and sleep. My mother would stay into the evening, consoling me and keeping an eye on Melina. The first night, I panicked when Ma got up to go home, so Aunt Lina offered to spend the night. I was in no position to refuse her offer; I was useless to myself and to my daughter. She stayed over every night for the first week I was home, sleeping in my bed with me while Michael slept on the couch in the TV room; the TV helped him sleep. Aunt Lina brought Melina's bassinette into my room, so she could be nearby if Melina woke up in the night.

Michael was distraught. This was not the homecoming he envisioned. He spent the afternoon before I came home assembling the crib and cleaning the house — his version of clean, anyway — and there I was, curled in the middle of the bed, a mess of hair and tears. He did not know what to do. He would have done anything to help me, but all there was to do at first was wait it out and hope things changed for the better.

Ma and Aunt Lina cooked supper and everyone ate. I sulked. Ma and Aunt Lina cleaned where Michael missed. I cried. Ma and Aunt Lina fed and changed Melina. I wept. All I wanted to do was sleep and cry. My inexplicable despair was all-encompassing.

"Let's look at the gifts, Sylvia," my mother called to me from the kitchen. I lay on the couch with a cold cloth on my forehead. It was hard to get up and down with the stitches in my belly. She came into the TV room carrying one of the many packages.

"Ma," I whined, "why? What's the point?"

"People went out of their way to get you and the baby nice things. You can at least look at them."

"Fine."

There were gifts everywhere, in every room, from friends, family, colleagues and customers. I was tripping over packages and cards and gift baskets. So many people loved us. It broke my heart to look at the gifts. I was grateful for the effort and the sentiment, but in my mind, I was still sure this motherhood thing was temporary. *What a waste,* I thought. *I don't want her. I really wish they had saved their money.*

"Oh, look at this little dress," Aunt Lina, in Italian. "Sylvia, isn't this pretty?" It was pink and ruffled, just like all the others.

"Yes, it's pretty," I said, barely looking up. My mind was focused on all the thank-you cards I would have to write, all the people I would have to call. I hated writing thank-you notes even when I was feeling good. What would I say now?

Dear Joan and Doc,

Thank you so much for the gorgeous outfit for Melina. You are so thoughtful. Too bad we had to give our baby away. She was just too small and we sent her back. I'm sure she would have gotten a lot of use out of it.

Sincerely,

Sylvia and Michael

Hi, Kate, it's Sylvia . . . Oh, I'm great. How are you? . . . Thank you so much for the layette set. It is just darling . . . Well, I'm sure she's fine, but I really don't know . . . Well, we had to give her back . . . Yeah, just changed my mind . . . Yeah, well, you know how it goes. Some people have natural maternal instincts and some don't . . . (laughing) Well, you have a great Labor Day, too. Don't get too much sun at the shore . . . Okay. Bye.

"Sylvia, Sylvia." Ma snapped her fingers at me, holding up a pastel-colored jelly ring. "Syl, look at these teething toys. Aren't they sweet?"

"Yeah, Ma, they're great."

After we opened some of the gifts, Aunt Lina called us into the kitchen to help give Melina a bath. At two weeks premature and barely over five pounds, she was way too small for the baby bathtub we had purchased. Aunt Lina decided to improvise. She rummaged through the pickled oak cabinets until she found it — my Aunt Stella's pink salad bowl. Aunt Stella was one of my favorite aunts and had died a few years before. Just seeing the salad bowl made me miss her. Aunt Lina filled the salad bowl with water, put it on the counter and plopped Melina down in it.

"What are you doing?" I asked her. *Is she crazy?*

"I'm giving Melina a bath."

"I can see that. But why are you using Aunt Stella's salad bowl?"

"It's the perfect size," she said, matter-of-factly. "Now here, hold her head." I put my hand under Melina's head while Aunt Lina washed her miniature arms and legs.

"But Aunt Lina, I love this bowl. Can't we find another one?"

"This one is fine. And it can be washed. Don't worry so much, Sylvia."

Just as the words "don't worry" passed her lips, Melina pooped in the bowl. Right there in Aunt Stella's salad bowl! I was mortified.

"You know what? She's too tiny. You take her. I mean it. You can have her." I took Aunt Lina's free hand, moved it under Melina's head and turned and walked out of the kitchen. I was furious and outraged. *How could she poop in Aunt Stella's bowl? Why was she ruining my life?* I continued up the stairs, into my room and slammed the door.

It was too much. I couldn't do it. Everything about her revolted me, and yet seeing the bowl, I was saddened Aunt Stella would never know my daughter. I resented her for existing, even though she was part of Michael, whom I loved so deeply. I was furious with a tiny, helpless baby, and hated myself for it. For the second time in one day, I cried myself to sleep.

"Sylvia, Janie is on her way over to see you," my mother whispered into my ear. She gently nudged my shoulder, trying to rouse me. "Do you want to come down?"

"Not really," I murmured grumpily.

"Syl, come down and say hi to Janie. You'll feel better."

"Okay." I relented without a fight. I was happy to see Janie; she's one of my dearest friends. We grew up together and had jointly faced all the trials of being children, teenagers and twenty-somethings. Now, faced with "grownup" problems, my friends were rallying again. Marianna promised to stop by too.

"I've laid some clothes out for you. Take a shower and change and come downstairs."

"All right. I'm getting up." It took all my strength to peel myself off the bed.

"Syl, you look great," Jane squealed as I came down the stairs. I knew she was trying to be nice, but it annoyed me to be humored.

"You don't have to say it if it's not true, Janie," I mockingly scolded her.

"I'm not. You do," she protested. Janie was always good for a laugh and I was really glad to see her. We hugged and took seats at the little kitchen table. Ma was in the laundry room and Aunt Lina was scrubbing the bathroom. They were always cleaning something.

"Do you want something to eat?" I asked. "Aunt Lina and Ma have been cooking as if the whole neighborhood is coming over. I can heat up something."

"No, thanks," she said. "I don't want to wear you out."

"Oh, you won't. That's what Melina is for." I tried the big-shot-as-long-as-the-baby's-not-around trick I learned in the hospital.

"Where is she?" Jane laughed.

"Sleeping," I said casually. "We'll get her up in a little bit."

"I can't wait to see her."

"She's great. She's just great. I still can't believe she's here." The bullshit piled up deeper and deeper the longer Jane was there. I bragged. I puffed. Everything was great. Nothing could be better. There was no pretending with Ma or Michael or Aunt Lina, but, for some reason, with Janie, even though we've known each other for over twenty years, there was no stopping me. I suspected she didn't buy my routine, but I kept it up anyway. We looked at more of the gifts, we chatted about formula and diapers, I inquired about her seven-year-old son, Sam, anything to keep from talking about what was really going on. We even had a laugh watching Ma and Aunt Lina in their XXXL housecoats zipping around, cooking and cleaning nonstop. They had so much energy. We sat there in awe and amusement.

Janie and I were still facing one another at the table, a little refuge in the kitchen filled with baby formula, nipples and gifts that wouldn't fit anywhere else, when all of a sudden, a stream of liquid spurted through my gray t-shirt, creating a huge wet spot.

"Did my tit just spit at you?" I was stunned.

"I think so," Janie laughed. "Do you have any breast pads?"

"No."

"Sweetie, you should get some. Until your milk stops coming in, that's just going to keep happening."

"God, it's always something, isn't it?"

"Yep. That's motherhood."

When Marianna stopped by later, she brought me some breast pads. She couldn't believe I didn't know what they were.

"I told you, Marianna, I was too busy to read."

"But no one mentioned it to you?"

"No. No one told me anything except, 'You'll know what to do when the time comes,' and 'Everything will be fine.' If one more person tells me everything will be fine, I'll scream.

Hell, I may scream anyway. I don't know what to do, and nothing is fine." Marianna just hugged me. She did not say everything would be fine.

Of all of my friends, Anna is the most label-conscious. When she showed up at my house a couple of days after my release from the hospital with preemie onesies from Kmart, I almost fell off the couch. Miss Not-Without-My-Prada had gone slumming.

"They're so cute, you'd never know," she said, defending her purchase.

"Thank you. They're wonderful." I meant it. Everything else we bought or received was too big for the itty-bitty Melina.

"I looked all over, but no one had any this small. You know, I wouldn't normally shop at Kmart, but you said this is what you needed most."

"You don't have to explain, Anna. They are really great. They'll fit her perfectly," I reassured her.

"So, what else did you get?" Anna, like everyone else, wanted to rifle through the loot. It was a reasonable request, and normally I would have shared her enthusiasm. Before Melina was born, I cooed over tiny shoes and little dresses. I oohed and aahed over fancy strollers and baby monitors, but now the gifts left me cold. I was immune to the charm of baby gear. Nothing was cute, nothing mattered. I was numb.

"Are those Gucci slippers? Oh, my God. They are so adorable!" Anna found the little booties one of my customers had given Melina.

"It's good that they're too small for you," I teased her, "or you'd sneak them right out of here."

"You know I would," she said, laughing.

I laughed, too, but I didn't feel any better. For all of my friends' efforts to lift my spirits, I was blue. No. I was less than blue. I was grey. All the life had drained out of me and I didn't know where it had gone. Into Melina? Out with the afterbirth? I wanted desperately to share my agony with someone, but I feared rejection and scorn. Most of all, I feared that admitting it would make it real. I prayed to God to wake me from my nightmare.

That evening, after everyone had gone home and my household was asleep, I crept out of my room and into the guest bedroom. I tiptoed over to the desk in the corner and switched on the computer. For an hour and a half, bathed in the blue glow of the monitor, I researched adoption agencies. I couldn't take care of her. She had to go.

Of course, there was Michael to consider. I couldn't ask him to give up his daughter. *Maybe something would happen. Maybe if I left the front door open, someone would take her. Children are kidnapped all the time.* The police station idea was sounding better every day. *I could just tell Michael I lost her. I lose shit all the time, why not the baby? Kids wander away, get lost . . . but she's too small. Damn it! She's too small to keep and too small to get rid of.*

The greatest disaster of my life was my fault. I wasn't ready. I didn't nest, I didn't read any books, and I didn't ask any questions. I never took the time to think about what motherhood would entail, what the ups and downs would be. Everyone sensed something was wrong, that *I* wasn't right. I created this terrible situation and everyone would have to pay for it, especially Melina. I wanted to hit rewind.

She didn't deserve me. Self-loathing and shame enveloped me. Tears dripped on the keyboard as I shut down the computer. *Sleep, give me some sleep.* I would worry about plans to get rid of her in the morning. Or maybe I would just sleep through the whole day, into the night. Daylight meant people were talking about me, about my failure. Maybe I could just sleep through the rest of my life.

The next day, I had a pain in my abdomen worse than any of the labor pains I screamed through the week before — I was constipated. I had never experienced anything that was actually gut-wrenching before, but this certainly was. Tears streamed down my face as I sat fruitlessly on the toilet. Before I left the hospital, Dr. Weiss said I may experience some constipation, and prescribed a stool softener for me, but I didn't think I would need it, so I didn't bother to get it. I had flushed the ones the nurses at the hospital gave me. I was suddenly regretting my decision to ignore the instructions of those many medical professionals. The pain was excruciating and I had to do something. I called Marianna from the toilet.

"I haven't been able to poop in 8 days."

"Didn't they give you anything in hospital?" she asked.

"Yeah, but I didn't feel like taking it. When they asked if I'd had a bowel movement, I lied."

"Sylvia, why did you do that?

"I don't know, I just did. But I can't stand the pain any-more." I was close to tears once again. "Do you think it would be okay if I left Melina sleeping and just ran out to the phar-macy?"

"No! You can't do that," Marianna exploded. "You can't leave a newborn alone."

"She's sleeping. She won't even know I'm gone. Besides, she can't get out of the bassinette by herself. It's not like she could hurt herself."

"Listen to yourself, Sylvia. You're talking crazy. You can't just leave her."

"Well, I don't care. I'm in pain and I'm going." I hung up on her, pulled up my sweatpants and went into the bedroom to change. I pulled on my jeans and threw on a T-shirt. Thank God for slip-on shoes — it was still hard for me to bend over. I jogged down the stairs and grabbed my purse from the table. Melina's bassinette was nestled in the corner of the den, where we moved it during the day. I peeked in at her one last time and, just as I was about to open the front door, she started wailing. I couldn't believe it. For hours she was quiet, but when I wanted to leave — when I needed to leave — she had to wake up. I was furious. I ran back over to the bassinette. I lost it, standing over her and screaming uncontrollably.

"Now, you're crying? Now? I can't believe this! What do you want from me? I can't believe this!" Who knows how long I stood there, venting my frustration and anger at my helpless newborn.

All of a sudden, Michael came running into the house.

"Sylvia, what is wrong with you?" he yelled at me. "You can't leave the baby alone. Why are you screaming at her?"

"I . . . she . . . I can't . . . I can't do it." I collapsed on the floor, exhausted and filled with shame. Michael sat down next to me and held me in his arms.

"I don't know what to do to help you," he whispered, "but I'll do whatever it takes. We'll figure it out, okay?"

"You're not mad at me?" I asked sheepishly.

"No, I'm not mad." He reached into his pocket and pulled out a small box. "Here, I brought you a present." I looked at the box and then up at Michael. It was a box of Fleet Enema.

"How did you know?" I cried in relief.

"Marianna called me."

My mom holding me

Eight

Seeking Escape

Postpartum depression is the most under-diagnosed obstetrical complication in America.

—Dr. Diana Dell, Associate Professor
of Obstetrics and Gynecology,
Duke University

Just as I was getting used to being home again, the out-of-town relatives descended. My mother was planning a backyard barbecue at her house on Sunday so everyone could meet Melina and we could all be together. The old Sylvia would have been excited about a party, but the new Sylvia was dreading it. I didn't know how I was going to face everyone. I couldn't look them in the eye and smile and say how great motherhood was when I just wanted to curl up and die — when I wanted to give Melina away.

"Sylvia," Michael nudged, "why don't you get out of the house for the afternoon. Go get a manicure. Have a spa day. It'll make you feel better." Marianna seconded the idea.

"We'll watch Melina and you can have a break. Tomorrow's the party, and you'll enjoy it more if you're feeling pretty." It was a good idea. I loved getting my nails done, and I certainly could use a respite from my worries. The salon had always done the trick. At my one-week follow-up the day before, Dr. Weiss said I shouldn't drive for two weeks, but having an afternoon out was too enticing. All the way to the salon, I tried to think about the peaceful manicure, relaxing pedicure and invigorating foot massage I would have, but I could only replay my frustrating postnatal checkup.

Marianna had driven me to my appointment. For ten months, I was a familiar face around their office and the folks on staff were eager to hear about my darling new baby girl. However, I was not in the mood to be chatty. I took a seat in the far corner of the peaceful waiting room while Marianna checked me in.

"Hi, Sylvia," the receptionist called out to me with a wave. "How are you?"

"I'm fine," I said curtly, averting her gaze. I did not feel like being my usual vivacious, talkative self. Marianna sat next to me and patted my hand. The receptionist gave Marianna a knowing glance.

A few minutes later, my name was called, as cheerfully as always.

"Sylvia, you're up." She looked at me eagerly, trying to elicit a smile.

"Thanks, Lisa." I nodded as I walked by, giving her a half-hearted wave.

"You're welcome, honey."

"Let's take a look at that incision, shall we?" Dr. Weiss got right down to business in his usual brusque manner. He lifted my blue gown and peeked at the gash across my abdomen. "The stitches look good. You look good."

"Well, I don't feel good." I had to fight back the tears. "Dr. Weiss, I'm really feeling depressed. Do you think there is something wrong with me?"

"Oh, Sylvia, it's natural for a new mother to be a little blue after giving birth. It's nothing to worry about."

"But I don't want to have anything to do with the baby. I mean, I don't want to feed her, change her — I don't even want to look at her."

"Don't worry about it, Sylvia, really. It'll get better. It's just the baby blues. After a couple of weeks, you'll be feeling good as new."

"Can't you give me something until then, some sleeping pills, something? I can't sleep, I can't eat. I just feel like shit."

"I really don't think you need medication, Sylvia. What you are going through is perfectly natural."

"But it's not just the blues. I can barely function. I just want to die."

"Sylvia, listen to me. A lot of new mothers go through a slight depression after childbirth, but it goes away. Trust me."

I couldn't believe he wasn't taking me seriously. I knew in my heart things were going to get worse, but I rationalized his reaction. He's a doctor. He's seen hundreds of new mothers. He would know if something is really wrong. Against all my better judgment, I left his office empty-handed and empty-hearted. Marianna was also disappointed in Dr. Weiss.

I pulled into the salon parking lot, snapping back to reality. Sitting in the car a moment to collect myself, I took a deep breath. This was going to be great. The owner and employees of the salon were Vietnamese and spoke little English, so conversation would be limited. There would be no questions about the baby, no inquiries about my new life. I could truly escape, or so I thought.

From the minute I poked my head through the door, I was verbally bombarded. The women who worked at the salon were normally very quiet and only talked to each other, but all of a sudden, they were chatty — chatty with me. The language barrier was no match for the curiosity and excitement surrounding the recent birth of my daughter. The salon owner and his wife were expecting their first child and wanted to know everything. Or I guess that's what they wanted. There was a lot of gesticulating and "sign language," but not a lot of communication. The peace and solitude I craved was stolen once again. I couldn't hide from her. Even the salon belonged to Melina.

I was ushered to a manicure station and a young woman began on my nails while the other women hovered around us. She put my right hand in a bowl of warm, soapy water and began asking me questions in broken English and Vietnamese. The others nodded and interjected, looking at me intently. If I had known what they were saying it might not have been quite so frustrating. I nodded and tried to smile. I said how beautiful Melina was and how glad I was to be home. I bullshitted about the miracle of life and beauty of giving birth. I still don't know if they understood anything I said. Slowly, they began to grow tired of me and trickle away. I concentrated on my hands. These hands had hardly touched Melina since she was born. Pretty soon, I was going to have to take on some responsibility for my child. My eyes welled up with tears as I took short, shallow breaths, trying to stifle my emotions.

By the time my manicure was over, I was feeling dizzy. I debated whether or not to flee, but I really wanted a pedicure. I was determined to relax. Once I was settled into the pink vinyl pedicure chair and my feet were in the hot, bubbly water, I felt better. I leaned my head back, closed my eyes and pretended to fall asleep. The salon melted away into the smell of peppermint foot lotion and the sounds of bland, soft rock on the radio. Peace at last.

The pedicurist tapped me on the shoulder when she finished polishing my toenails and asked if I was ready for my massage. I opened my eyes to her outstretched hand offering to help me out of the chair. I could not stay there another minute. From every angle, the mirrored walls reflected my haggard self and I couldn't take any more cheerfulness from the staff. I made up a story about a forgotten appointment and made my escape. My flip-flopped feet carried me out of there as fast as they could. I fretted all the way home about my failed mission. Peace and quiet continued to elude me. Even alone in the car, I couldn't escape the buzzing in my head. Upon my return home, Michael greeted me with a hug.

"Do you feel better?" he asked. I almost lost it.

"Why is having a baby such a big fucking deal to everybody?" I screamed. "Why does she have to be the center of the universe?" Michael stared at me in silence, as if he'd never seen me before. I guess he hadn't; I certainly wasn't myself. Then he wrapped me up in his arms and held me while I cried.

·   ·   ·

Ma and Papá came over that evening, excitedly detailing their plans for the party the next day and their upcoming cruise. That's when it hit me — they were leaving. They were leaving me with this little burden to bear all alone. Aunt Lina was still staying over, and would stay as long as I needed her, but it wasn't enough. My mother was going away. They were going to be gone for three weeks. I might be dead — Melina might be dead — by the time they came back. I burst into tears for the millionth time in a week.

"Sylvia, we can stay if you need us to," Ma reflexively offered. Papá started to protest, but was caught in my eyes. His expression changed from exasperation to sympathy and concern in an instant.

"Whatever you want us to do, we'll do," he said. "We'll stay if you need us."

"Please, don't leave me," I whimpered. I didn't know if I felt guiltier for asking them to abandon their vacation plans or for needing them in the first place, but the thought of them being more than a ten-minute car ride away for several weeks was terrifying. I needed them more than any of us knew at that moment.

"We'll stay, baby," Ma assured me. "Don't cry, my love. Don't cry. I won't leave you."

Nine

Party Girl

New parents quickly learn that raising children is kind of desperate improvisation.

—Bill Cosby, entertainer and comedian

The welcome home party arrived sooner than I wanted it to. I dallied in bed longer than usual that Sunday morning, letting Michael get up and take care of Melina. He had been working long hours at the restaurant while I recuperated, so I figured he'd want to spend as much time as he could with the baby. Even though I had skipped church, I asked God to send a rainstorm to postpone the gathering. My prayer went unanswered as the sun mockingly streamed through the bedroom window.

When I finally dragged myself out of bed, I took my time getting ready, hoping that Michael would just forget I was there and go on to my mother's without me. I fussed with my long black hair, I applied and reapplied my make-up to my unusually pale skin, I changed my clothes six times. I didn't really care what I looked like, I just didn't want to go.

"Sylvia, are you coming?" Michael called up the stairs to

me. It was about 1:30 and I was standing in front of the full-length mirror on the back of our bedroom door, trying to muster the courage to face my family. "We should get going. People were supposed to get there at 1."

"Did you get Melina ready?" I asked, fully aware of the answer.

"Yep. I put her in the little teddy bear jumper and she's all set in the carrier. We're just waiting for you."

"Did you pack the diaper bag?" I stalled.

"Yes, honey. And I made three bottles. There are diapers, wipes, toys." He paused, presumably to take a deep breath. "Syl, we're ready. Just come on so we can go!" Michael yelled, impatiently.

"All right. I'll be right down," I hollered back. *You can do this*, I told myself. *These are your friends, your family, people you love. And who love you.*

Music and laughter spilled from my mother's backyard, beckoning us to join the festivities. The sky was cloudless, clear and blue, and though it was the middle of August, the heat of the sun had yet to overstay its invitation. The smell of charcoal and wood chips mingled with the sweetness of the honeysuckle blossoms that flanked my parents' driveway — it smelled like summer. I took a deep breath and, for a moment, the familiarity was comforting.

Ma loved throwing parties and, as usual, she and Aunt Lina had gone nuts. There was enough food to feed the forty or so guests several times over. People were gathering around the redwood picnic table situated near the edge of the yard under the canopy of perfect sky. My father stood at the grill overflowing with filet mignon. He forked a hefty chunk of meat and flipped it over, the juices sizzling on the hot metal. Ma was bringing another tray of my father's famous home-made mozzarella and bread down the steps of the back porch to join the huge platters of grilled vegetables and ten-layer Sicilian lasagna already on the table. Michael's parents brought jugs of their homemade wine; I made a mental note to keep away from that stuff.

We came around the side of the house and, the moment I saw the crowd of people, my blood ran cold. There was no getting out of it. I had to face them. My cousins had come from Florida to see Melina. I had to produce a happy baby, a happy mom and a picture perfect life. I took another bracing breath and walked right into the middle of the gathering.

"We're here!" I announced with as big a smile as I could muster.

"Sylvia. Michael. Where have you been?" Ma asked, making a big show of our arrival. "We were getting worried about you."

"We're still adjusting to the routine, Ma," Michael defended us, laughing. "It's our first big outing. Cut us some slack." It wasn't the first time Michael had made excuses for me since Melina arrived, and it would not be the last.

"Well, let's see that baby," Josephine gushed. "Oh, Sylvia, you look great. So slim already."

"Thanks, Jo. I'm down from mammoth to baby elephant," I joked. *This isn't so hard.* "Wait until I can wear my pre-baby jeans. Then you can get excited."

A chorus of "Oh, she's so beautiful," and "She looks just like you," among the Italian exaltations, rang out above the music blaring from the boom box on the porch. I was glad they liked her. *Somebody should*, I thought. I started mentally adding names to my ever-growing list of potential surrogate parents; there were plenty of moms in this group. *She should have one who loves her.*

One great thing about massive family gatherings and a new baby is you never have to hold the baby if you don't want to. And I didn't — have to or want to. I ducked out of the mob of people clamoring for my week-old daughter's attention and snuck into the house. The bathroom was my refuge and strength. I would be safe there. I splashed some water on my face, patted myself dry with one of Ma's fancy mauve guest towels and sat on the toilet lid to plot my escape. *Maybe I could just leave and no one would notice. They all just wanted to see Melina, anyway. No one would miss me. I could just run away.* That was it. Suddenly, I felt twelve years old. I could just run away. *I have a little money. I could go to another town where no one would know me. They would have no idea I had abandoned my family. I would just be Sylvia, not Sylvia Lasalandra, restaurateur, wife of Michael Frodella and mother of one tiny child. I could go to the city. People escape to New York all the time. In a city of 8 million people, no one would notice me at all.*

"Sylvia, are you okay?" Aunt Lina's voice interrupted my fantasy.

"I'm fine. I just needed to splash my face," I answered. *Damn it. Aunt Lina is like a hawk and she would fucking find me.* I opened the door and Aunt Lina put her chubby arm around my waist.

"Come back outside, sweetie. Everyone wants to see you." She led me out onto the porch and found a seat for me in a shade-covered lawn chair. Several cousins gathered around me. "Now, give her some air, ladies," Aunt Lina scolded. "I'll fix you a plate, Sylvia."

"It's okay. I'm not really hungry."

"Nonsense," Aunt Lina called back, halfway to the table before my protest completely left my lips.

"You need to keep up your strength," my cousin Donna said. "With that little bundle of joy to take care of, you need to stay strong."

"Right," I sighed. So this was it. This was my life. And it was all about Melina.

The hours dragged by and I did my best to make it look like I was having a good time. I chatted with cousins and made small talk with my friends. Every now and then I noticed Michael checking on me. He would peer over his shoulder, mid baseball conversation with my brother Nicky or discussing the finer points of the Jets' roster with Nicky and my other brother, Jimmy. When he caught my eye, he'd give me a wink and go back to the boys.

I watched my sister-in-law, Kim, proudly showing off her newborn, Martino, to the family. Our babies were just a month apart in age, but Kim and I were light years apart in mothering ability. Sure, she was on her third, but I'd helped with her older two. *Why can't I be as together and confident as Kim?* I could feel myself growing resentful. It wasn't Kim's fault I felt like the gum on the bottom of someone's shoe, but seeing her negotiate the rigors and the joys of parenting with such skill and precision was doing a number on my already fragile self-esteem. I tried once more to sneak back into the house.

"Hey, Syl," my friend Kelly called out as I made my way up the porch steps. "I'm going in to change Morgan. You want to help?" She came up behind me with her 11-month-old daughter under her arm. Morgan giggled as she kicked and twisted, trying to escape her mother's grip.

"I guess so." Morgan's pacifier fell out of her mouth into the grass as they crossed the yard. I froze with panic. *She dropped her pacifier. What should I do?* I ran down the steps and picked it up. It had some grass clippings from the freshly mowed lawn stuck to it. I stood there at a complete loss. *Should I sterilize it, or just throw it away?* I wondered.

"Thanks, Syl," Kelly said, as she took the pacifier from my hand, wiped it on her jeans and stuck it back in Morgan's mouth. I looked at her with horror. "Don't worry, Syl. You'll get used to it." She smiled and took my hand with her free one and led me inside.

I sat in the rocker in my old bedroom while Kelly changed Morgan's diaper on the bed. I was in awe of her ease and her calm when it came to motherhood. I envied her casualness. Kelly had always been easygoing. She was artsy and fun; she made her living as a graphic designer and was always doing something creative. She lived by her instincts, and she made being a mom look like the most natural thing in the world. Everyone said it was, but watching Kelly, I actually believed it. She made me feel, just by her actions, that everything would be okay for me, that I could do this. I felt relaxed for the first time since we brought Melina home.

"Kelly," I ventured, "this has been harder than I ever dreamed it could be." My heart pounded with the prospect of confession. "Did you ever think you weren't cut out for motherhood?"

"Sure, Syl, everybody thinks that." She smiled and looked me squarely in the eye. "But it gets easier, I promise."

I appreciated her words of encouragement, but I couldn't

believe them. That's what everyone said, but with each day my life grew harder. My coping mechanism was shutting down and I felt closer and closer to the brink with every hour that passed. It seemed like the more I wanted to be a good mother, the harder the tests were. It reminded me of the saying about God not giving you more than you can handle. *Does he think I'm made of steel?* I knew I had a breaking point and I hoped something would change before I reached it.

It was well into the evening when the last of the relatives said their goodbyes and made their way to their homes. I was spent. I lay on the peach and teal sectional sofa in my mother's family room with a cold rag on my head. Michael was packing up some leftovers with Ma in the kitchen, while Papá rocked Melina to sleep in the recliner next to me. I peeked at the pair of them from under my washcloth. Papá didn't hold us much as kids, but there he was, gently whispering a lullaby to my baby daughter. *He should keep her,* I thought. *He's better with her than I am. Much better.*

Mom and Poochy

Ten

On the Brink

Left untreated, postpartum depression can degenerate into postpartum psychosis. Symptoms include auditory hallucinations, visual delusions and suicidal, even homicidal, impulses.

The afternoon sun streamed through the second-story window of our bedroom, keeping me awake, but I couldn't get up to close the curtains. My limbs were stuck to the mattress, my head like a lead weight to the pillow. *Which is heavier,* I thought, *a pound of feathers or a pound of lead? She is so tiny, a pound of feathers would do it.*

My mind began to drift. *Michael is at the restaurant . . . no one would know. She's brand new . . . This happens all the time . . . I could do it and no one would know . . .*

My heart pounded in my chest, my hands clenched the downy, white comforter. The white walls began closing in . . . closer and closer . . . so much white. Panic and pumping blood filled my skull. The pounding grew louder and louder.

I felt my body shift until my feet almost reached the floor. The faint sound of whimpering trickled into my ears, competing with every tick of the clock. I lay back with my toes just touching the fluffy, aqua carpet. My socked feet would make no sound. Slowly, I pulled myself up. The light from the window was warm on my face, but I felt cold — cold and empty. A hollow shell. *I used to have everything a successful woman could want. Now it means nothing.*

Our house was situated on a corner made by two busy streets, but the room was silent. I felt like I was in a vacuum: no sound, no air. The baby lay peacefully in her bassinette, but I still could not relax. I hadn't been able to rest since we brought her home. *Had it only been a week? Was the party really yesterday?* It seemed like an eternity. I tried to sleep, but every time I closed my eyes I only saw horror — the baby, a pillow, my hands. I lay back down on the bed and stared at the ceiling, my heart beating faster and faster. *It would be so easy*, I thought to myself. *So easy . . . It's her fault. She did this to me. She came here uninvited and took away my life. She sucked the blood from my veins, the marrow from my bones and left me like a conch on the sand. If you put your ear to my heart, you can hear the white noise of nothingness.*

I felt myself stand and, when I looked back at the comfy, iron canopy bed, the bed that used to be a refuge, I saw myself, the worthless woman I'd become. I used to have a purpose. I used to have joy. I was the life of the party, and every other cliché you can use to describe an energetic, vibrant person. I used to take care of people. I used to love, to be fun. That Sylvia was gone, and I didn't know if she would ever come back.

The crying grew louder and, as it filled the room, echoed down the block and through the town. I knew it was up to me. Only I could stop it. I hated myself for what I had to do. So did Abraham. So did Judas. But they did what they had to do because it was their destiny. *This is mine.*

I picked up the pillow from the bed that nearly filled the room. It would be over soon. I would have my life back. I could start over, like nothing had happened. We could go back to before. My fingers gripped the edges of the pillow and, without my conscious will, my feet moved slowly to the lacy, marshmallowy bassinette, so soft, so cozy; cradling her, comforting her in ways that I could not. The pillow in my hands pulled me across the room like a divining rod to water, guiding me to the source of my pain, of my worthlessness. I stood at the foot of the bassinette, afraid to look inside. If she saw my face, she would know. I closed my eyes tightly and waited. Minutes, hours, days passed as I stood at the foot of her tiny grave, where she would sleep forever, peacefully, never to know the failure of her mother, never to feel the pain of life, the despair it brings.

The crying stopped. It was done.

I bolted upright in bed, sweat dripping into my eyes, my hair in a tangle. I jumped to the floor and ran to the bassinette. Melina was there, sleeping peacefully as usual. In the week she'd been alive, she rarely cried; I did her crying for her. Tears streamed down my face. *What was I thinking? What was I doing?*

"It's okay, little one," I reassured her. "Everything will be okay." The words rang falsely in my ears. She turned her head slightly, but remained asleep. She knew what I wanted to do. I turned my back on her, unable to bear the shame. She had to know. She knew I didn't hold her, but maybe she didn't know why. I didn't know why. "Everything will be okay... Everything will be okay..." I kept repeating the phrase through my sobs, hoping that the more I said it, the more I would believe it. It wasn't working.

I padded over to the grey nightstand on my side of the bed. Mine differed from Michael's in content only. Valium, Ambien, Zoloft, and Percocet littered the tabletop. I stared at the bottles, squinting through the bright sun flooding the room, marveling at how I got here.

I finished university in less than three years, summa cum laude; I married a wonderful man who was my best friend; I had a wonderful family and good friends; and I opened and operated two successful restaurants. Yet there I stood next to my nightstand, ready to end it all. This was not supposed to happen. Depression was not a luxury I could afford. I worked hard for everything I had. And now, none of that mattered. Nothing mattered anymore. I was isolated and desperate.

Sitting on the edge of the bed, I emptied all the bottles onto the creamy white comforter my mother gave us for a wedding gift. I got lost in the tone-on-tone brocade pattern. The swirls and spirals spun and popped. I ran my fingers through the multicolored pills that sprung up like flowers in a garden — blue, purple, pink, yellow — pretty colors. They felt cool and calming to the touch. The sound of the little plastic-coated pellets bouncing off one another was soothing to my addled brain. I picked up a handful. I was ready.

Melina sighed and stirred in her fluffy little cocoon. My mind snapped to attention and I looked over to her corner of our room. She just lay there sleeping. She never cried. She was perfect and good. I hated her. Tears burst from my eyes and the pills cascaded to the floor. My heavy sobs forced me prostrate on the bed. I had no more control. Somewhere along the way I lost my grip and I had no idea how to get it back.

I can't do anything. I can't even kill myself. I can't do this. I just want to be alone. I just want to crawl out of my skin and slink away. I don't want her here. I can't look her in the eye. If I do, she'll know what a miserable excuse for a mother I really am.

Something in my head clicked. I pushed myself up from the tangle of sheets and pillows and sat on the edge of the bed. As if in slow motion, I reached over to the phone on the nightstand and began to dial. With each push of a button, I could feel my salvation coming.

"Ma," I choked into the receiver. "Ma, I can't do this." The sobs returned in a flood. I rocked back and forth on the bed. "Please, help me," I gasped.

"I'll be right there," she reassured me in her heavy Sicilian accent. "Sylvia, don't do anything stupid, okay? Do you hear me?"

"I hear you, Ma. I won't do anything, I promise." I meant it.

"Don't go anywhere. I'm on my way."

"Okay, Ma. Thank you." I slowly put the receiver back in its cradle and sat on the side of the bed, just staring out the window. The sky was crystal clear, blue and bright, the opposite of what I felt inside, where only blackness and rain loomed. If my sense of humor hadn't been sucked away and spat out like snake venom, I would have laughed at the irony, at the beautiful late-summer day as it mocked the perpetual night in my head.

I was frozen on the edge of the bed, staring out into the world. I felt like a prisoner in my own home, in my own room, in my own body. And there lay the warden, sleeping quietly. *Why doesn't she ever cry? Why can't she be colicky and frustrating?* At least that might justify my agony. But she didn't, and she wasn't. I had no excuse to hate her. *Where is the maternal instinct I was promised? What is wrong with me?*

Barely ten minutes had passed when I heard my mother's footsteps growing louder as she lumbered up the stairs. The tiny, round woman scurried into my bedroom and, without a word, flew to the bassinette and picked up the sleeping baby. Melina woke up, but still didn't cry. She nestled her tiny, black fuzz-covered head into my mother's shoulder and went back to sleep.

"It's okay, baby. It's okay," Ma comforted Melina. Then she looked into my eyes. "It's going to be okay, my baby." She bounced with Melina as she walked over to me and took my hand.

"Sylvia, I'm taking Melina home with me. Your father and I will keep her as long as we have to, until you get better."

"But Ma, what if I never get better?" I was stunned by my mother's generosity.

"You will."

"But Ma, what about Florida? What about your cruise?"

"Sylvia, family comes first. I couldn't live with myself if I left you now, now that you need me."

The tears returned in a gush. As the only daughter among four sons, I had never been the recipient of my mother's undivided attention and devotion, and yet, now that I was at the end of my tether, she was here, ready to put her own life on hold to save my life and my daughter's.

"I'm sorry, Ma. I'm sorry. I didn't know it would be like this. I never thought it could be like this."

"I know, my baby, I know." She sat next to me and put her arm around my waist and squeezed me tightly. "Now, I want you to rest. We will talk later about what to do."

I heard more footsteps pounding up the stairs. Michael appeared in the doorway, out of breath, catching himself on the jamb with his large hands. Ma got up and walked around

the bed to him. She took his hand and led him into the room.
If she had been tall enough, she would have tousled his wavy
black hair.

"Ma, I came as fast as I could. Is she okay? Honey, are you
okay?"

"Everyone is fine," Ma said. "I'm taking Melina. You stay
with Sylvia and don't leave her alone. I am trusting you with
my daughter's life, Michael."

Michael walked over to my mother. At 5 feet 11 inches, he
towered a foot above her head. He bent down and kissed
Melina softly on the head and wrapped his arms around my
mom.

"Thank you, Ma. Thank you." He stood and looked at me
from across the room. I could see his heart break before my
eyes. The guilt and shame of my failure was almost too much
to bear. I collapsed on the bed in a puddle of tears and sobs.

Michael ran around the bed to my side.

"Syl, it's going to be okay. We will get through this. I
promise. We will. I'm not going to leave you alone. It's going
to be okay." His voice was soft and comforting. His arms
encased me. Together we rocked back and forth, and he
stroked my hair. "I love you."

My mother walked around the bed to where we sat and
kissed my forehead. She looked into my eyes and gave me a
sweet, little smile accompanied by a wink. For the first time
in weeks, I smiled, in spite of myself.

Eleven

In Search of Relief

Women suffering PPD need to be medically tested and prodded until the physical cause of their symptoms are found
and treated.

—Sylvia Lasalandra, PPD survivor

After my horrifying brush with psychosis, my family,
along with Marianna, gathered to discuss what to do.
We agreed that Melina would stay with Ma and Papá, Aunt
Lina and her daughter-in-law Anna. Marianna would stay
with me and take charge of my mental health regimen. She
was furious that Dr. Weiss had ignored my pleas for help and
for her suggestion that I be put on medication for my depression. As a psychologist, she knew what was wrong, but, as
my friend, she was unable to treat me herself. She told him
about my symptoms — loss of appetite, sleeplessness, depression, and, of course, the thoughts of suicide — but Dr. Weiss
insisted my "blues" would pass, and felt I required no other
treatment. Marianna knew differently. She recommended
a colleague, Dr. Dickenson, and accompanied Michael and
me to my first appointment a week later.

Dr. Dickenson's office was professional, but welcoming. The off-white walls and gray carpeting were a touch sterile, but the furniture was comfortable. Michael and I settled in on the black leather couch, with Marianna to our left in a matching chair. Dr. Dickenson rose from behind her massive cherry desk and took a seat in another chair opposite the couch.

I shuddered at the sight of her. She was a petite, Latina woman with long, dark brown hair, perfectly pleasant in appearance and demeanor — and seven months pregnant. *Oh, God*, I thought. *How can I tell her what I want to do?*

The tears started before I could say a word. Michael and Marianna gave Dr. Dickenson the rundown of our situation. She nodded and jotted down notes, giving me looks of pity and mild concern. When I could finally speak for myself, I explained in my own words.

"I want to give up my baby. I can't take care of her and she deserves more than I can give her." All the while, I stifled the urge to scream, "Don't have your baby. You can have mine!" She patiently listened to me repeat, "I don't want her. I don't want her."

"Sylvia, don't rush into this decision. Putting your baby up for adoption is a drastic measure. When the depression passes, you will likely regret your decision."

Depression? I thought. *This is more than the depression. I want to get rid of my baby before I kill her!* My sobs prevented me from voicing my rage.

"Of course, we know that," Michael explained. "But Sylvia is sick. She can't cope. Adoption is certainly the last resort, but if that's what we have to do to make her well . . ." His voice broke and he dropped his head, unable to say the words. I realized Michael really would do anything for me, even give up our baby. My guilt and shame compounded.

Marianna interjected that perhaps some medication was in order and Dr. Dickenson agreed. She prescribed 10 milligrams of Prozac and, as she closed her pad, tried to reassure me that everything would be okay. Before we entered her office, my hopes for recovery were low, and, as she sent us on our way, to pharmacy and home, I felt little relief. I believed no one could help me, not Michael, not Marianna and certainly not this pregnant doctor.

In the subsequent visits with Dr. Dickenson, I found her to be professional, clinical and certainly not as sympathetic as I had hoped. I was on my own for the most of the sessions and did most of the talking. She nodded and scribbled and interjected little.

"Sylvia, you are in no frame of mind to be making this kind of decision," she said when I told her for the hundredth time I wanted to get rid of my baby. "Time and medication are going to get you through this."

"Just because you're a doctor doesn't mean you know how I'm feeling," I snapped. "I've been taking the Prozac, but I don't feel better, just numb."

"You have to give it time."

Time was something I didn't have, at least with respect to the doctor. She would be leaving to have her own baby in just a few weeks and I felt rushed to get better before she left. I couldn't understand why the drugs and the therapy weren't helping. Deep down, I knew I wanted my baby home, if not for me, then for Michael, but the progress was not going quickly enough.

In our second session, Dr. Dickenson mentioned postpartum depression for the first time. She didn't say I had it, but she mentioned that my symptoms were similar: loss of appetite, fatigue, restlessness, not feeling connected to the baby. She upped my medication and suggested that perhaps I consider hospitalization. That got my attention.

"You think I should be committed?"

"I think, if you don't progress, if you remain a danger to your self and your baby, it could be a viable option. Of course, it would be voluntary."

Voluntary? I'd seen enough fried calamari in my time to know I didn't want to have my brain fried. The thought of being institutionalized terrified me even more than I was already. I couldn't function in the "real" world, but I did not want to be locked up, for my own good or not.

When Michael told her of the doctor's suggestion, Ma flew into a frenzy.

"Once a 'crazy,' always a 'crazy,'" she reasoned. "I don't want her in a place like that, with all that depression and hopelessness, where a toothbrush is considered a weapon. She'll lose hope of ever getting better if she is branded now. She'll think she is weak, and she's not."

The stigma surrounding mental hospitals was very real for her. My parents grew up in a time and place in which psychiatry was scorned. It was hard enough for them to accompany me to a shrink, but it let me know just how committed they were to my recovery.

Marianna agreed that hospitalization was an extreme solution and remained active in my at-home recovery. She called me four or five times a day and checked in frequently with Dr. Dickenson. The doctor mentioned to Marianna

I shouldn't be left alone, so she and her husband Chip, and even their dogs, Indiana and Jones, added babysitting — me, not Melina — to their already busy schedules. One morning, I was awakened by the deadliest stench. I opened one eye to discover Jones staring at me. Her breath cut right through 10 milligrams of Ambien. She definitely got me out of bed that day.

I had round-the-clock care from my friends, family and coworkers. Aunt Lina continued spending the nights with us and was, for all intents and purposes, our live-in nanny while Ma and Papá cared for Melina. The attention and doting was too much and not enough. I craved my freedom, but I also wanted help — the right help — and I was sure, if I ever got it, I would be better in no time.

After four weeks of treatment with Dr. Dickenson, I went in for my last session. Michael and my parents accompanied me. The anxiety could have been cut with a chainsaw. I wasn't fixed and I didn't know what I was going to do. None of us knew what to do. The thought of starting over with a new therapist was draining the little emotional resources I had left.

Dr. Dickenson encouraged me to begin reincorporating Melina into my life by visiting her before work and, eventually, taking her home. My throat felt like it was closing up. Visiting Melina would mean eventually having her overnight, and it was more than I could bear. Ma started to tell the doctor I wasn't ready, but stopped and quietly listened, biting her tongue. I knew Ma was right, but I could see by the look on Michael's face that he was of a different mind. He sat there, still in his chef's coat from the restaurant, with his hands jammed in his pockets. He looked at Ma with a look I'd never seen before — it was hate. If I had been in my right mind, I would have strangled him right there.

My father held himself together for as long as he could before he broke down in tears. His little girl was sick, the son-in-law he adored was full of rage, and he was helpless to fix either of them. Dr. Dickenson certainly had her hands full that day. I'm sure she was desperate to be rid of the whole messy lot of us. Maybe that's why she recommended Dr. Tulipano.

My session with Dr. Tulipano lasted all of twenty minutes. The doctor was a Latina woman in her mid-50s with a thick accent. Her office was drab and gray. She was very friendly as we entered the office, but I remained ill at ease.

My mother came along for moral support and to have some of her questions answered. I gave her the laundry list of my problems: my baby was living with my mother, I couldn't emotionally or physically take care of her and I was having horrible thoughts of killing her and myself. She listened patiently, sitting stiffly behind her desk. When I finished, she stood up, walked around the desk and sat on the front edge facing me. She leaned in and looked me directly in the eye.

"Mrs. Lasalandra, when you leave here I want you to go to your mother's, get your baby, take her home and start bonding with her."

I couldn't believe my ears. Had she been listening to me? I just said I wanted to kill my baby!

My mother jumped up from the couch as if spring-loaded and, cursing in her broken English, went for the jugular. She grabbed Dr. Tulipano by the shoulders, pointing and shouting that she was crazy and trying to kill both Melina and me.

"You a fake!" Ma screamed, pointing at the degree on the wall. "That license is a fake! You not really a doctor!" I had to pull Ma away, kicking and screaming, and drag her out of the office.

"Let's go to the IHOP," Ma said as we escaped to the parking lot. "That bitch make me so mad, I'm starving." That was the first time I laughed since Melina was born. No matter how rough things were, Ma was always thinking about food.

I was in turmoil. I didn't know where else to turn. Three doctors failed to see the seriousness of my illness and I was still no better than I was when I left the hospital. I forced myself back to work just three weeks after Melina was born in hopes that the distraction would take my mind off things. I found, however, I was just as zombie-like in my little office above *Bruschetta* as I was at home.

Michael and our crackerjack staff had been keeping the business running smoothly, and I was glad to be back — at first. I thought I would be glad to see my customers and my friends, but I found I wanted hide. I thought making the last-minute preparations for *Bacchus* would get me excited about something again, but my enthusiasm quickly faded. Everywhere I looked, I was faced with the reality that I had a child I'd rather not have.

The storage room at *Bruschetta* was filled with baby gifts; the house was filled to the brim and we needed the extra room. Every time I passed the stock room, there were cute, pink, safety-featured reminders of the biggest mistake of my life.

My employees were surprised I was back so soon and were full of questions I couldn't answer, at least not out loud.

"How's the baby?"

The baby is a terrifying parasite.

"How does it feel to be a mom?"

I feel desperate and panicky.

"Isn't motherhood great?"

Motherhood sucks.

My office above the kitchen usually kept me away from the rest of the staff, but on my first few days back, I was the center of attention. I just wanted to be alone. I learned quickly to make my entrances and exits through the side door to avoid facing anyone.

My coworkers dropped by my office periodically to check on me.

"Sylvia, can I get you anything?" JoJo asked.

"No, I'm fine."

"Is something wrong? Do you want to talk?"

"No, really. I'm fine."

"Okay. If you need anything, just holler."

I wasn't fine, I just couldn't talk about it. Saying it out loud made it real. Admitting my failure was admitting there was something inherently, instinctually wrong with me. Mother's are supposed to bond with their babies. The joy of parenthood is supposed to compensate for the pain of childbirth, but bonding and joy were two things I was lacking.

As with everything else in my life, our restaurant was a family affair. Aunt Lina and my older brother Jimmy made all of our pasta by hand from a small room across from my office. Melina was there beside Aunt Lina in her portable playpen. Day after day, Aunt Lina made pasta and Melina listened for me. Whenever I passed by the open door, she would gurgle and coo with excitement. She knew I was her mother and she wanted my attention, but I could barely look at her.

Aunt Lina would say, "There's your mommy, Melina." and Melina would smile at me. Nodding and half-smiling, I would run into my office and hide. No matter how I tried to ignore her, she was always happy to see me, clamoring for a glance from her mother. I wanted to be happy to see her, but no matter how cute, no matter how bubbly, I was not interested. From the corner of my eye, trying not to get her hopes up, I snuck the occasional glance at her. She was like any other baby — small, pudgy, helpless. I had to look away to keep from crying and get out of there as quickly as possible. The baby smell grossed me out, and the thought of getting any closer made me nauseous.

She was such a happy baby, never colicky or fussy. There was no reason I should have been averse to her existence, but I was. Retreating to my office, I would sit there and stare at the toffee-colored walls for hours. I couldn't concentrate on work, but I also couldn't admit it to anyone. I was afraid if they knew I couldn't work either, they would just tell me to go home and be with the baby. I couldn't do anything.

Jimmy often tried to make little jokes with me when I would pass through. One of our favorite things to do together was watch "Mad TV."

"Ms. Swan make you some really good farfalle today, Ms. Sylvia," he would say in the character's voice. I couldn't laugh. I couldn't even look at him, or anyone. My coworkers tried to talk to me, to cheer me up, to understand, but I was closed off to their efforts. Everything seemed hopeless and out of control. And just when I didn't know where else to turn, I had a visitor.

Father Michael Carnevale was the first person I confided in who didn't make me feel like less than a mother. The fact that he was a Franciscan priest did not intimidate me; he spoke in everyday language and made everyone feel special. I could even curse as much as I wanted. He was dynamic and person-able. He came to visit me at work one evening when I was feeling my lowest. I was a faithful member of the St. Mary's congregation, and our history enabled me to tell Father Mike, without fear of judgment, that I didn't want Melina and that I'd thought of killing her and of killing myself. Nothing I said shocked him. In his eyes, I *was* a real mother and a good person; I was a parishioner and a friend.

"Sylvia, God loves you," he said. "You have support in your faith and in your family."

"But how? I've given up the responsibility of the perfect baby God gave me. How could He still love me?"

"God is not frowning on you, Sylvia. He doesn't think less of you."

"I want to be a good mother, but I can't. No matter what I do, I just can't look at her. And I have so much shame. I mean, my mother is taking care of my child."

"Sylvia, when I heard you and Michael were having a baby, I knew in my heart you'd be a good mother. And you are."

"Yeah, right."

"I'm not joking. A mother makes sure her baby is taken care of, and that's exactly what you are doing. By giving Melina to your mother, you are doing what a good mother would do. You are making sure she is fed, cleaned, housed and loved." I had never thought of it that way.

"God still loves you and knows you are doing the right thing for Melina. She may not be living at your house, you may not be giving her primary care, but by recognizing your inability to provide for Melina, you are doing right by her. And by God."

"But everybody thinks a baby should be with her mother. And, for some reason, they don't mind telling me."

"Fuck what people think." I smiled at his impassioned slip. "You have to do what you have to do to get yourself healed so Melina can come home. Through faith, you will find the strength to heal."

"I pray everyday for that strength."

"And it's there, inside you. God will provide it."

I thanked Father Mike for his trouble and he reassured me his was an open door. I felt, for the first time in months, that I was a valuable human being.

After two unsuccessful tries at recovery by psychotherapy, I was very wary of the third referral, but emboldened by Father Mike's words, and, at the insistence of Marianna, I gave it one more shot.

Dr. Nowak was a tall, dark-haired woman in her early 40s, and a colleague of Dr. Dickenson. In the first ten minutes of our first session, I knew all I needed to know about her — she had already looked at the clock twice.

I talked and she nodded, but I sensed she didn't really hear me. I was quickly losing my patience and my faith in the medical community, but I didn't have the energy to seek further assistance. I asked for prescriptions for sleeping pills and antidepressants and she complied. Our relationship was established and would continue in the same manner for several months.

For a while, I continued making weekly trips to her office. I would talk, she would feign understanding and interest. There was little in the way of counseling. If I told her I was feeling worse, she would up my dosages. Numb and emotionless, I floated through my days. When I expressed this to Dr. Nowak, she said in her monotone voice, "Well, at least you're out of harm's way," as she looked at her watch.

Oh, I get it. Being a zombie without the energy to kill myself is better than being suicidal. That's a way to live. I had really had it with her. She was using me for an easy paycheck, so I began using her as a dispensary. I would tell her I was feeling better, and she believed me, or said she did, and would cut our sessions short. I would lie and say she forgot my Ambien prescription last time, and she would give me another. I would take one scrip to CVS and one to Drug Fair.

Eventually, I stopped going to see her altogether and just called in my prescription requests. She always complied, never questioning me as long as I came in for a monthly maintenance session. I began doing my own research at home, reading everything I could get my hands on.

The sad truth was there was precious little information

available. My trips to the library, to Borders, to Barnes and Noble, were mostly fruitless. The Internet yielded little by way of useful material. Luckily, a family that refused to let me go down without a fight surrounded me. The round-the-clock supervision continued and, if I knew nothing else, I knew I had people who would die trying to keep me alive.

At Melina's Christening:
Dad, Mom, Melina, me and Michael

Twelve

Godmother Knows Best

Having a child gives you the opportunity to fall in love in the most profound way. It's not always love at first sight, but as you get to know this human being, you fall in love in ways you never knew existed; it is completely unconditional.

—Kelly Gray, Melina's godmother

It was our family's third Christening in two months; we'd had a busy, baby-filled summer and fall. My nephew, Martino, was christened in August; my niece and god-daughter, Lara, was christened in September. I questioned Johnny's judgment about my fitness to be Lara's godmother, but he insisted. Now, it was finally Melina's turn. I had hoped I would be "fixed" by the time October rolled around, but it was not to be. My sentence as an emotional prisoner was dragging on and nothing much had changed.

Michael and I met my parents at their home a couple of hours before church to dress Melina and take pictures. Melina looked so sweet in the creamy white christening gown my mother bought for her. Her soft, black hair curled daintily around her tiny face. Her shining eyes sparkled as they searched for mine. I looked away, unable to meet her gaze. Michael wore a new gray suit and blue tie. He looked so handsome, his thick, chestnut hair combed neatly back from his dark eyes. Suddenly, I wished I had bothered to get a new outfit for the occasion instead of wearing the black skirt and short, rust-colored jacket I threw on in haste that morning. As with most things I used to love, I just could not bear to shop. I kept saying to myself, "Why bother? We won't have her much longer anyway."

Michael took Melina from her car seat, his eyes filling with tears as we walked hand in hand up the steps of the church. There was a knot in my stomach the size of a melon and my hands were shaking. Although I knew there was nothing to be afraid of, I was terrified. St. Mary's Church was gorgeous, and packed to overflowing the day of our celebration. Autumn flowers of gold and orange filled the sanctuary. Family came from all over and, of course, all my friends were there.

As we walked down the flower-laden aisle, all eyes were on us. No amount of concentration could block the whispers from filling my ears. I gritted my teeth and held my head as high as I could. They couldn't say anything that would make me feel worse than I already did. We took our place in the front few pews and waited for the service to begin.

Kelly, who would be Melina's godmother, took Melina and held her. Michael, on my other side, held my hand. His parents were in the row behind us. I was afraid to look back and see Mom's face. She was trying to understand what was happening, but the tension was there and felt by everyone. I had let so many people down. The guilt and shame were nearly crippling.

Father Mike presided over the ceremony with his usual humor and zest. In the time since Melina's birth, Michael and I had met several times to seek counsel from Father Mike about our unique situation, and he remained supportive and committed to help us. I felt safe with him. There was at least one person in the room not judging me.

My faith in God has always been strong. Even in my darkest hours, I knew that God would, somehow, take care of me, of us. As mass began, a choir, seemingly of angels, filled the church with glorious music. I closed my eyes and let the sound wash over me and prayed for a miracle.

Kelly gave me a nudge. It was time to take Melina up to the baptismal font. We stood and walked to the front of the church. Michael's brother Angelo stood as Melina's godfather. Father Mike gave a lovely speech about the miracle of life as a gift from God. *Some gift*, I thought. *Maybe He takes returns; she's hardly been used. Now's the time, God. If You just take her now, we can all go back to the way things used to be.* He didn't take her. Or me.

Then Father Mike took Melina from Michael's arms and held her high in the air. "Please welcome into our fold, Melina Lasalandra Frodella." The congregation jumped to its feet and applauded for our little girl. Instead of overflowing with joy and pride, I withered and withdrew just a little more into my shame.

The reception was like no other since my wedding. Italians know how to throw a party. The Princess Chateau Hall was filled to overflowing with over a hundred guests and enough food to feed three times that many. Laughter and music spilled out of the hall as we approached with the guest of honor. Already, or still, I felt self-conscious and paranoid; it was a feeling that was becoming normal. Michael did his best to keep up appearances, but I knew he was torn apart inside. I despaired for him and our little girl, who, through no fault of her own, was being deprived of her mother.

When we arrived at the hall, people were already mingling. It felt like every eye was on me as we passed through the gathering crowd. It was as if the world had gone into slow motion. I was in a tunnel of face and eyes. Mouths shouted congratulations and whispered gossip.

"Is the baby home with her mother yet?"

"Oh, my God. She lost so much weight."

"I can't believe her baby isn't home with her. A baby needs her mother."

I wanted to shout back, "Listen, you assholes, I can hear everything you are saying. I have postpartum, I didn't lose my hearing," but when I opened my mouth nothing came out. Michael shepherded me into the reception hall like a celebrity plowing through paparazzi.

The reception was festive and happy for most in attendance. The 100-plus guests feasted on catered, upscale Italian cuisine and danced to the favorites only a hired DJ can spin — like a wedding reception, but with a baby. I tried to stay clear of the wine for fear of blabbing all my troubles to anyone who would listen, but thanks to Dr. Nowak, I was so heavily medicated, I found it hard to connect to anyone. I found a quiet spot in the corner and watched the party like a wallflower, only this wallflower didn't care if she was asked to dance.

All I could think of was the gossip. I could feel people talking about me, even when I couldn't physically hear it. I was shocked at how cruel some people could be. Most everyone in the town new our baby was with my parents, and though people knew what I was going through, it didn't stop them from saying mean and hurtful things. I call it the CC, Cruel Chatter (or sometimes Clit Chatter, because most of the culprits were women). I had even considered many of them my friends or supporters. Opinions flowed as freely as water, whether or not the bearers knew the details of my depression or even had children of their own.

"Do you think she is really sick?"

"I don't understand why she just can't snap out of it."

"Do you think she is just doing this for attention?"

For crying out loud! I wanted to stand on the banquet table and shout, "If I really needed your fucking attention, I could flash my double-Ds for you right now! That'd give you something to talk about. Do you really think I woke up and thought, 'Hey, I need some attention today. I know, I'll to try to kill my baby, and if that doesn't work, I'm next.'?"

Luckily, everyone at the party was spared my striptease of revenge when Kelly took the stage. The DJ called the room to attention and gave Kelly the floor. Michael found me in my corner and, taking my hand, led me through the crowd. Ma was holding Melina and gave me a little wink as we approached.

"Ladies and gentlemen, the godmother," the DJ announced, handing Kelly the microphone.

Sylvia, Michael, thank you for honoring me with the responsibility of being Melina's godmother. Having children gives you the opportunity to fall in love in the most profound way. It's not always love at first sight, but as you get to know this new human being, you fall in love in ways you never knew existed; it is completely unconditional. I am glad that Sylvia and Mike decided to become parents and take on the hardest and most rewarding job that any human being can have. I have known Sylvia for more than 20 years. Our friendship has withstood the test of time. We are always there for each other, no matter what. We give each other advice, hard truths and a lot of laughs. As Melina's godmother, I promise to be there for her when she needs me, and even when she thinks she doesn't. Sylvia and Mike have been blessed with this beautiful little girl and, as their friend, and now as Melina's godmother, I am blessed."

Applause filled the hall. It really was a beautiful speech, but for the second time that day I doubted I would ever understand what the fuss was about. Everyone says a baby is a miracle, that the love of a child is greater than any you will ever know; that children are blessings, but my clouded mind could only question those concepts. *How can a baby be God's little miracle when my baby caused me such pain and despair?* Maybe they were all crazy and I was the sane one.

Thirteen

Psycho Mama

Around the world, about 600 mothers kill their children each year, most typically with water, pillows or pills.

—Robert R. Butterworth, psychologist.

Even after months of half-hearted treatment by doctors and round-the-clock care from my family, I was still haunted by thoughts of killing my baby and myself. Every time I saw water — driving by the lake, filling the bathtub, washing the dishes — I could see myself holding her under until she faded away. Pillows were lethal weapons, able to block the air from her tiny lungs until she went quietly to sleep. The only method I rejected was giving her pills. The pills were mine, and I was not about to share. For all my horrible visions, somewhere, deep down, I was concerned with Melina's wellbeing. I didn't want her to grow up thinking she caused her own mother's death. No child deserves that kind of burden and, though I could take her or leave her, I wanted her to grow up free of the guilt and shame that was keeping me in bondage.

I knew in my heart that if I succeeded in taking the life of my daughter, I would be next. Luckily, my Catholic fear of hell, and the drug cocktail from my psychiatrist, kept me from acting on the constant impulses to end it all. "You've been so good your whole life," I would tell myself, "don't fuck it up now." Still, if I had had Dr. Kevorkian's number, I would have called him.

Michael wasn't convinced that my religious convictions were enough to keep me alive. One day, Marianna called him at work in a panic.

"Michael, I don't think Sylvia should be left alone."

"What do you think she'll do?" He shared her fear.

"Suicide is not out of the question." She spoke the unspoken at last. Michael was out the door before the receiver had settled into its cradle. That night, and every night that followed, he returned from work, sprinting up the stairs to our bedroom to see if I was still alive. He lived in fear that he would come home one day to find me dead on our bedroom floor. Out of this fear, Michael got in the habit of hiding my medication, but I would hoard pills like a squirrel, in case I wanted to kill myself later. I kept little piles between the clothes in my dresser drawers, stashed away in the closet, in the ashtray of my car. Just knowing they were there made me feel safe. All I had left were the resources to kill myself.

During the day, I was fidgety and restless. I took the Prozac that made me feel empty, numb and gave me nasty headaches, but mostly I longed for the night. Not only did the night quiet the voices of the people I was sure were talking about my haggard appearance and lousy parenting skills, but the Ambien was there for me. At night, I could take two and drift off into a peaceful sleep — the only peace I could find.

If I woke up, I would take two more, whatever it took to keep me from facing the reality of my life.

The line between what was real and what was fantasy was becoming blurry. I heard things that weren't there. I often heard my front door open, even when I knew it was locked, sure that people were coming in to spy on me. Sitting alone in my room, voices told me that things would never get better, that I should act now. *It will look like SIDS*, the voices said. *No one will believe it was you.* Sometimes, the voices forgot about Melina. *Sylvia, you have so many pills . . . Just take them all and your suffering will be over.* Not even my constant sobs quieted their taunting.

Knowing I was on the brink, Ma and Aunt Lina never let me out of their sight. Those two sauce-covered Italian mamas were up my ass all the time, following me around in their XXXL housecoats, thick white socks and complimentary slippers from Al Italia, each with a mop or a broom in hand and their eagle eyes trained on me. I was enrolled in the Lasalandra 24-Hour Sicilian Daycare until they said not. No matter where I went in the house, Ma was there. My friends, even Michael, thought she was babying me unnecessarily, but I needed her to. I was like a child again. I only ate if she made me. I only got out of bed if she made me. I only took a shower if she made me.

On more than one occasion, she burst in on me while I was in the bathroom, particularly if I was in there for a while. One day, I was seeking refuge in the cool quiet of the lavatory when I was overcome with a flood of tears. Ma must have been lurking in the hallway just outside the door. It only took one loud sob for her to waltz in.

"Oh, I didn't know you were in here," she lied, proffering her mop. "I was just going to clean up a little."

"Ma," I sobbed with exasperation. "Just leave me alone."

"Okay," she said, glancing down at the magazine basket on the floor. "Oh, look. They find Elvis. What you think about that?" She sat down on the edge of the tub and picked up *The National Enquirer.*

"Ma, Elvis is dead," I shrieked, falling into her lap.

"Oh, my baby." She cradled me in her arms and rocked with me and stroked my hair. "I'm not going to leave you. I will be here as long as you need me. If it takes another month, another year, or 10 years, I will be here."

And that's how it was. Ma and Aunt Lina, with the help of my cousin Anna, took care of the day-to-day operation of my household. Ma frequently cooked my favorite dishes. I ate more eggplant with plum tomato sauce that year than I have in my life. Aunt Lina kept my house spotless. Anna cared for Melina as if she was her own child. I would sit in the kitchen for hours and do nothing while they swept and scrubbed, polished and buffed around me. They were always busy, always watching, slyly, from around the corner, from behind a book. Although I knew it was for my own good, their constant presence was aggravating. If I protested, I was always met with resistance. Ma was willing to piss me off, to piss Michael off, my in-laws, anyone, to ensure my safety. There was no place I could hide. My every move was monitored for my own safety.

When I was able to go back to work, Ma would come over in the morning and help Lina with breakfast. Knowing I wouldn't eat, she made me a concoction of Marsala wine, sugar and egg yolk.

"Here, Sylvia, drink this. It gives you energy." I would go to work a little tipsy from the wine and high from the sugar.

When Michael came home from work at night, a meal and Melina were waiting for him. Ma and Papá tried to make sure Michael got to spend as much time with his daughter as possible. It was so hard on him to be separated from her, and he was grateful for every minute he could be with her, at our house or theirs.

My parents' house was a short drive from ours, but a world apart. My mother's decorating taste was what I like to call Italian French Provincial. The light blue velvet couches in the living room were covered in clear plastic, and provided an unobstructed view of the 60-inch television set. Until about 10 years ago, the carpet was eye-popping orange shag. Coupled with the sky blue sofa, it was meant to evoke a beautiful sunset. It mostly invoked a headache. In the corner, next to the fireplace, was a life-sized *David* replica that Ma took great pains to adorn for holidays. Every room was filled with Italian glazed porcelain knick-knacks, Capodimonti, and every room contained a TV no smaller than a football field. The one in the family room was 72-inches. It was like a Cineplex. Melina's bassinette was on wheels so Ma could roll her easily on the white ceramic tile floors between the family room and the kitchen.

As time went on, Michael and I began visiting Melina at Ma and Papá's more frequently, though I was carefully chaperoned. I was treated like the little cousin who might drop the baby on its head, and rightly so. I was allowed to hold her and look at her, not that I really wanted to do either, but I was never permitted a solo audience with my own child. If I were alone in a room with Melina, Ma would come in and pretend to dust the countless Capodimonti just to watch me. If we were all spending the afternoon together, Ma would watch me from behind a book. I'd see her face peek out from behind the pages and hear, "Lemme see how you hold the baby."

Even Poochy was on Melina watch. Poochy was Ma's ancient poodle. He weighed about 4 pounds, had lost most of his fur and had only one testicle. But what Poochy lacked in physical attributes, he made up for in, well, balls.

"Now, Poochy," Ma would say, "don't let anyone near Melina, especially Sylvia. That's your job." And he would comply.

During one of the first afternoons I spent with Melina at my mother's house, I walked over to the bassinette to peek in at my baby. Poochy jumped up from his spot at the skirt of the tiny bed and barked his little head off. I was so startled that I jumped back, more out of surprise than fear. This pathetic little dog was committed to defend Melina to the death, and though it wouldn't take much to accomplish that feat, he was ready for a fight. There was nothing to do but laugh.

"Ma, if you really want to keep me away, I recommend a Doberman," I joked.

"You hurt my Poochy, and I will kill you myself," Ma snapped back. Even in the face of darkness, my mother never lost her sense of humor. She knew I needed a constant, and she was one by just being herself.

. . .

Though I spent most days in the company of women, my brothers were also keeping tabs on me. They knew I didn't want their pity and were never intrusive, but they let me know, each in their own way, they were there for me.

Nick, busy with his own growing family, called Ma and Papá regularly to check on me. Occasionally, we chatted on the phone and he reminded me what a great aunt I was.

"The kids are nuts about you, Syl. You know that, right?"

"I know, Nicky. Thanks."

"I just want you to know how special you are."

My youngest brother, Dave, is a quiet guy, and he often came over to Ma's just to sit and watch TV with me. He loved to hold Melina, and though he knew I still couldn't, he would always ask, out of respect, if I wanted to take her. Just that little gesture let me know that he and I were on the same page, that if I needed him, he was there for me and Melina.

Jimmy, who I saw frequently at *Bruschetta,* would try to make me laugh or simply smile at me whenever he caught my eye. He was always cracking jokes to cheer me up, but knew how far was too far and never crossed the line. No act was too small or went unnoticed. Throughout my ordeal, I knew if I said the word, my brothers would be there, ready to fight for me to the death.

While my other brothers kept a healthy, respectful distance, John tried to pull me out of my depression kicking and screaming. One morning, he showed up at my house and insisted on taking me to lunch. There was a restaurant in East Rutherford known for its great wine cellar and, under normal circumstances I would have been thrilled with the invitation.

"No, Johnny. I don't want to go," I said, flopping down onto the chair in my TV room.

"Come on, Syl. It'll be fun," he pleaded, taking my hands and trying to pull me up. "You need to get out of the house. A little liquid lunch will do you good."

"Really, Johnny, I don't feel like it." I jerked my hands from his grip.

"Well, how about some shopping then? That always makes you feel better." He paused for a moment, and looked me squarely in the eye. "I'm not taking 'no' for an answer."

I didn't want to disappoint him. He was trying so hard to help me. I finally agreed to let him take me to lunch. Though he had gotten me into the car, I could muster no excitement about the outing. I kept wondering why he wanted to spend the day with me. I was no fun anymore. *Maybe he won't want me to be Lara's godmother,* I thought. *That would be a load off. I can't even take care of my own kid, let alone someone else's.*

We drove in silence. I didn't feel like talking and John didn't know what to say. We arrived at the Riverside Square Mall. John was hungry so he decided to eat at this French sandwich shop. John ordered a tuna sandwich and some things he knew I liked, hoping I would have at least a nibble. When the food arrived, I just stared at it. John was very observant of my behavior and didn't press me to eat. He tried to engage me in conversation, but I remained silent. Part of me wanted to be a good sister and friend, but it couldn't override the part that could barely get out of bed. The more he attempted to draw me out, the less I responded, so he tried another tack.

"You know, Syl, you need a haircut. When's the last time you went to the salon?

"I don't remember."

"Well, then. We will fix that."

As we walked through the mall looking for a salon, John was chatting about this and that. I just kept walking and wished for the day to be over. Johnny was trying so hard, but I was in agony. He finally found a salon, and a Russian woman wearing a black smock over her black jeans and T-shirt greeted us.

"Hi. My sister needs a haircut." The stylist smiled and offered me a seat in a black vinyl barber's chair. The whole place was very black and cold, like my mood.

"You don't look so happy," the stylist commented, making eye contact with me in the mirror.

"I'm fine," I snapped.

"Okay. What would you like today?" she asked.

"I really don't care. Just cut my hair."

John looked at me like I had three heads. I am usually not that rude, on top of being very anal about my hair. I have always kept it long and never want more than a trim. This time, I didn't care what she did.

"Well, I guess a surprise could be good," John said in shock.

"Seriously, do whatever."

"Okay. We'll give you something nice. Not too short, but you definitely need a new shape." The stylist was trying to be accommodating.

"Fine."

She flung a black drape across me and got to work. John flipped through a magazine, occasionally looking up to check our progress. The stylist tried to make chitchat at first, but I didn't respond.

"She's not feeling well today," John explained. "Don't take it personally." She shrugged and continued working.

When she was finished, she held out the hand mirror for me to look at the back.

"It's fine. Whatever," I said, standing up without even checking her work. She took off about 5 inches. I would have freaked out if I had been in my right mind.

"Syl, you look great," John said, still a little stunned that I was so blasé about my precious hair. It was just above my shoulders, shorter than I'd worn it in years.

"I don't care. Take me home"

John paid the stylist and gave up. There was no making me feel better. We walked silently to the car and drove equally silently back to my house.

"Syl," John said as I got out of his car, "you really do look great."

"Thanks, Johnny." I gave him what little smile I could. "Really."

"Anytime." He smiled with understanding in his eyes. He knew I wanted to have fun again, and he knew that I would. We all just had to be patient.

Since Lara and Melina were only a month apart in age, Johnny and I often met at the pediatrician's office to take the girls for their checkups. Ma and Aunt Lina always came too. I was not allowed to drive alone with Melina anymore than I was permitted to be alone in a room with her. Ma was sure I'd drive us off a cliff.

The waiting room was filled with functioning families, and I wished I could be a part of one. On the "well" side, the mothers and fathers played and read with their kids while they waited. On the "sick" side, kids clung to their parents for comfort, and they received it. I longed for that kind of connection with my own daughter, but instead, I was the ill child who needed reassurance. Ma gave my knee a little pat to remind me she was there.

When Melina's name was called, her entourage accompanied her into the examination room. Johnny waved Lara's little hand and wished us good luck. Ma waved Melina's hand back and gave them a wink.

As the doctor poked and prodded her, Melina looked to me for salvation. There was nothing I could do to make the visits more bearable. Her big silver-blue eyes searched for mine, but I couldn't watch. Ma sang and soothed her while I sat frozen, as helpless as she was. Aunt Lina made faces to make her smile. I felt so guilty for not being able to ease her anxiety, which only added to my own. *Why am I even here?* I wondered. *I'm just making things worse.*

With two clean bills of health, we piled in our cars and met at my mother's favorite post checkup lunch spot, IHOP.

"Come on, Syl. You should eat something," John said as he unfastened Lara's car carrier. Wordlessly, I got out of the car and followed my family inside. The hostess showed us to a big booth by the window.

"Your waitress will be with you shortly," she said with a smile.

I sat down by the window so I could look out. Ma put Melina's carrier on the table in front of me. Melina looked at me hopefully, trying to catch my eye. She wanted my attention so desperately. I panicked.

"I can't eat," I wailed, bursting into tears. "I just want to go home." I felt every eye in the restaurant on me. I jumped up from my seat and ran out to the car and cried. When I didn't return, John came out to check on me.

"I'm just so useless, Johnny," I sobbed. "I can't do anything for her."

"You are doing the best you can, Syl." He tried to reassure me. "Listen, Melina has lots of people around her who love her. She has a father, grandparents, aunts and uncles, even cousins, who love her and are here for her. Just think, Melina and Lara are going to be like sisters."

"Don't you understand? I don't want her."

"Sylvia, when you're better, you'll be able to take over, but in the meantime, Mommy, Aunt Lina and Anna will take care of her for as long as you need. Joe and I will do everything we can to help you. We are not going to let anything happen to you or Melina."

Even with the 24-hour support and surveillance, the simple, everyday things that I had taken for granted became strenuous chores. Taking a shower, making my bed, even going to the bathroom, became so difficult that I would break down at the thought. Some days I lay in bed sobbing because I knew if I got up, I would have to brush my teeth. Hygiene was a low priority, but it didn't matter, I was disgusting on the inside, too.

I managed to keep up the pretense of going to work for a while. Work was my escape from Ma and Lina, but I was certainly not productive. I used the opportunity to just be alone. I whiled away many a day just driving for hours. Once, I ended up in Pennsylvania before I realized I was even in the car. I would make trips to the market and then sit in the parking lot for 45 minutes, not able to get out of the car. I would follow Skyline Drive, its twisting turns and sheer drops beckoning me. A flick of the steering wheel could have ended my misery, but something kept me from going over the edge. Eventually, I couldn't even muster the strength to drive anymore. I was certain that people, even people in passing cars, were so angry and repulsed by me that I could barely leave the house unless it was an emergency, and, after a while, chocolate was the only emergency.

One day, I went to the Stop & Shop around the corner without brushing my teeth or my hair, as was becoming my habit. I meandered around the store indecisively, handling every candy bar, each bag of individually wrapped chocolates. I settled on Hershey's Kisses and took my quarry to the counter. The cashier watched and waited patiently as I dug in my pockets to find my money. Several moments passed as I waited for her to complete the transaction. She continued to smile.

"What the hell are you looking at?" I barked, glaring at her. "Haven't you ever seen someone buy chocolate before?"

"I am just waiting for you to give me the money in your hand."

I looked down, and there in my grubby paw was a crumpled $20 bill. I didn't even realize I was holding it. Mortified, I didn't respond, not even to say thank you. Polite to the end, the cashier passed me my change and I fled in embarrassment. Once home, I ran upstairs, ate about a dozen Hershey Kisses, climbed into bed, shoes and all, and fell asleep.

My physical health was declining along with my mental state and outward appearance. I was losing weight rapidly. I could barely eat and I was frequently evacuating green bile. When

I did manage to eat, it was usually the chocolate I kept hidden in secret stashes around the house. I was afraid if Ma or Michael found my hiding places they would take the chocolate from me. There was no reason they would, but I trusted no one, especially not Michael. I blamed him for my pain. Our relationship had been so strong before. We were best friends who relished one another, who shared everything, but the stress was dividing us. My silence, my distance, my constant despair rendered Michael helpless. His impatience and his frustration sent me deeper into my cocoon of isolation. He only wanted his daughter and wife back, but to me it felt like hatred. Doctors were telling us to bring the baby home, and he couldn't understand why I wouldn't listen to them He felt I was deliberately stalling, being selfish and enjoying the attention, but he couldn't really know what was going on in my head. There were times I wanted to hurt him for hurting me. I fantasized about beating him with the autographed Mike Schmidt baseball bat I kept in the closet, but I knew bloodstains would devalue my trophy. He repulsed me, and the feeling was mutual. Where I had once been wild and independent, I had become nearly catatonic and completely dependent on him. My rage was building and so was his. I was sure Michael found me disgusting, and I was ashamed for changing, for not being the woman he married. He was in constant pain, too. It killed him to see me suffer and be unable to help me.

Things were getting worse between Michael and my parents, as well. Ma and Aunt Lina were always under foot; our house was not our own. He wanted his life back as much as I did. The difference was, he wanted the new life and I wanted the old one.

Fourteen

No Rest, No Relaxation

Many partners are frustrated because they feel it's their fault
or their responsibility to "fix" or take the problem away. She
really just needs you to listen.

—Sylvia Lasalandra, PPD survivor

Michael and I decided to take a vacation, just the two of
us, to my parents' winter home in Florida. We hoped
it would help us to be away from the stresses of baby and
business. Michael tried to convince me things would get
better in time, but I didn't believe him. His frustration was
growing and there was nothing I could do to ease his mind.
It seemed as if our lives would always be a tangle of hurt and
resentment. Though we were together, just like we used to
be, we were alone, alienated and estranged.

My parents' condo was a sight to behold. Their home away
from home was a shrine to "modern" Italy. The eighth-floor
corner unit had views of the ocean in every room, and the
entire place was tiled in peachy Italian terracotta that my father and my brother Jimmy laid themselves. The walls were
made to look like hand-smoothed plaster, giving the space

141

the air of a mausoleum. In every corner there was statuary of fish, dolphins and seafowl. My mother loves her Capodimonti.

In the master bathroom, which was small enough to wash your hands in the sink while sitting on the toilet, my father had installed a homemade bidet for my mother. Basically, it was a kitchen sprayer attached to the sink through a hole in the vanity. Even on vacation, we had all the comforts of home.

Though not decorated to my taste, my parents' oceanside retreat was a tranquil respite, except for one thing: the palm tree floor lamp. Among the glass and brass end tables and display cabinets, it stood in the corner of the living room next to the white overstuffed sofa. It was the teal and pink of South Beach, and only required a touch of the finger to turn on and off. Just looking at it made me more depressed, and I fantasized about throwing it off balcony. When my mother called to check on us, I told her how much I hated that lamp. The next time I visited it was gone.

Along the path between the condominiums and the ocean was a beautiful gazebo that provided a gateway to the ocean. On our first evening there, we sat silently, watching the day fade into twilight. The beach had always been my favorite retreat, but I felt no solace in the sea breeze or the breathtaking vista.

"If we give Melina up for adoption, will you leave me?" I finally asked. Michael looked at me as if I had just cut out his heart with a butter knife.

"No, Sylvia, of course not," he replied. The pain and disappointment in his eyes betrayed his words. He was trying so hard to help me and I continued to let him down. He was devastated that I would give up Melina. The restaurants, the house — nothing we accomplished together could ever equal the success of a child, of a happy family, and it was beyond his comprehension that I wanted to throw it all away. Michael often cried in private at the thought of giving up our daughter, afraid that she would grow up with different parents, without us. He wanted to be a family, to go out to dinner, to take vacations, just the three of us.

"Sylvia, I just want you to know that we are in this together. I will help you in any way that I can."

I was speechless, so touched by those words. It was beyond my comprehension that he still wanted to be with me. I had changed so much from the woman he married.

That evening, we went out to dinner at the *Prawnbroker Grill* family-style restaurant we often frequented on our visits to Hutchinson Island in Florida. Cozy, with its dark wood furniture and trim and hunter green appointments, my favorite part of the décor was the collection of paddle fans that adorned the high wood-beamed ceiling. Each one was unique and beautifully crafted.

Our waitress approached to take our order. Michael had the mahi-mahi and, for some reason, I asked for the Cobb salad. It was something I never usually chose because it was more food than I could eat. It made perfect sense to order it now, when I couldn't eat at all.

We sat in quiet agony until our food came. The waitress popped in and out of our non-conversation, filling our glasses and bringing bread and, finally, our meals. She quickly learned to direct her questions and suggestions to Michael. I ignored her every time she stopped by. It wasn't personal, I couldn't even talk to my husband.

Michael kept staring at me, like he was looking for something. I pushed my food around with my fork, trying to avoid his gaze. He took my hand from across the table and forced me to look at him. For the first time ever, he didn't see the eyes he fell in love with. My eyes were empty, my soul was stripped from my body. He was married to an empty shell.

"Will I ever get my girl back?" he asked. "You are my soul mate, my motivation. I'm so afraid of losing you, Syl. What can I do to help you?"

Numbness took over my whole body. This was a question I could not answer. The thought of living another day seemed an impossibility, not to mention ever being my old self again.

"I don't know, Michael." I hung my head in shame. "I just don't know."

We barely spoke the rest of the trip. Evenings were spent with take-out pizza and salads in front of the TV. If we went out at all, it was for a quick bite and then back to the room. Sundays were easier. Michael watched football in the den and I curled up on my mother's bed and watched whatever caught my eye. With the TVs on, we didn't have to face the fact that we were unable to help one another, and, when even the television became more than I could handle, I retreated to the gazebo and sat for hours, silent and motionless. As I looked out over the vastness of the Atlantic, I pondered the best way to escape the hell I'd created.

We returned from our vacation more defeated than before.

Tensions continued to escalate between Michael and my parents as well, and I felt terrified by their fighting. Michael was jealous of the way Melina responded to my father. He knew it should be him she giggled and cooed for. It was so out of character for him — he was not a jealous person — but given the circumstances, his reactions were understandable. He began to despise me and blame me for his pain.

Caught between them and my own suffering, I knew I was completely responsible for the war at home. It pushed me closer to ending it all. *Melina would be better off without me, and so would the rest of my family. If I was gone, Michael could have Melina back and he could go back to being friends with my parents.*

I wanted to love him again, to care for him the way I used to, to be attractive to him and attracted by him. He was the love of my life and I was beginning to hate the sight of him. I held him responsible for my situation, for pressuring me and for not getting it. Yet I was keeping him from his daughter. I was the reason his family was a mess. That did not stop him from also blaming my mother. Deep down, Michael knew that they were helping, that my parents were doing what was best for all of us, but a schism grew between them that I feared would never be bridged or repaired.

Doctors were telling us to take Melina home, but Ma insisted on keeping her. It was the doctors' words against my mother's. It was only natural that Michael would feel conflicted. A doctor has a degree; my mother was a housewife. A doctor sees many patients and can draw from case studies; my mother can only draw from her own experiences. A doctor is objective; my mother only has our interests at heart.

My mother-in-law didn't help matters either. Michael's parents are of the same generation as mine. Also Italian immigrants, the families have much in common, but they saw things very differently when it came to Melina and I. Of course, my mother-in-law meant no harm, she just didn't understand the danger we were in. After Ma had been taking care of Melina for a month or so, she got a phone call.

"Carmella, Melina should go back with Michael and Sylvia. A daughter belongs with her mother."

"Sorry, Sue, I'm not taking that chance. Sylvia is sick and she can't take care of Melina. You can hate me if you want to, but my first priority is my daughter and granddaughter. I don't want a new baby, I raised five already. But my daughter needs me. You are welcome here anytime. I am not trying to keep you from your granddaughter. I am not trying to keep Michael from his daughter. I am only trying to keep Sylvia and Melina alive."

My mother kept her door open to Michael's family. They visited occasionally, however, they felt a child's place was with her mother, no matter what. They could not understand that my mother's motives were pure. Ma and Papá did not want to be full-time caretakers. They were about to retire to Florida and live a life of leisure. The last thing they wanted was to start a new family, but they did because they knew they had to. Had they carried on with their plans, I have no doubt Melina and I would be gone.

My parents loved Michael and he loved them. My mother always said he was everything she ever wanted in a son-in-law. Michael used to love going to Ma's. They would sit up late at the kitchen table and swap recipes and cooking techniques. But, eventually, he only tolerated visits so he could see Melina. Finally, the resentment built to boiling point.

"Ma, you have to let go of the baby. She should be home with us," Michael shouted at my mother.

"Michael, if you take the baby home, you'll lose them both. Can't you see that?" Ma countered.

"You won't give her a chance to try." Michael's face grew red and sweaty. "The doctors say Melina can come home. Why are you fighting it?" My father stood up and confronted Michael face to face. Well, sort of. Michael is at least a head taller than Papá.

"She's not the woman you married. She doesn't talk, she doesn't eat. If you get her better, you can have her back. If you keep pushing her to take the baby home, you'll regret it." Michael and my father stood toe to toe, if not eye to eye.

"Michael, listen to me, don't be una testa di cazzo. Don't be hard headed," Ma said, coming between them. "You have to trust me. I promise you this on the grave of my sister Stella, if you are patient and let Sylvia get better, you will have everything you had and more."

Finally, it hit home. Everything was on the line — our business, our marriage and our family. We had to work together if we were going to keep it all together. I was ready to give up everything, but Michael, like my parents, is a fighter. He began seeing a therapist at Marianna's suggestion. It was good for him to have someone to talk to — to hear just his side. He learned that he shouldn't feel guilty for wanting Melina back, for wanting me back. Everything he was feeling was perfectly normal. The therapist encouraged him to be direct and not to hide his feelings. He was trying to be so strong, but I knew he ached for me. His spirit was being crushed under the weight of my problems.

Fifteen

The Witches of Eastwick

Call it a clan, call it a network, call it a tribe, call it a family.
Whatever you call it, whoever you are, you need one.

—Jane Howard, journalist and writer

My family was desperate for me to be well again —
how much, I did not really fathom until my mother
and aunts held me hostage me for an evening.

Ma called me to say that Aunt Tina, her older sister, wanted
to see me.

"She just wants to pray with you, Sylvia. Aunt Lina and I
will go with you."

Aunt Tina is a very religious woman, just like the rest of
my family. During my illness, many of my relatives lit candles
and made little shrines in their homes dedicated to my recovery. I knew people all over our parish were praying for me.
It was a reasonable enough request to pay my aunt a visit, so
I grudgingly agreed to let my mother drive me over.

The car ride was quiet, not the norm for my mother and
Aunt Lina. They alternated asking me banal questions and
making chitchat. I answered them just as blandly.

"How are you feeling today, Syl?"

"Fine."

"Good. Good."

Silence.

"Did you eat today?"

"Yeah, a little."

"Good."

Silence.

"I like your hair like that."

"Ma, I didn't even comb it."

"Oh, well, it looks nice."

Silence.

Aunt Tina moved into Aunt Stella's house when she passed away, and, like most old-school Italians I grew up around in New Jersey, she spent most of the time in the basement. The upstairs is for company, the downstairs is where one lives. It's like having two houses in one: full kitchen, bathroom, living room and bedrooms on each floor. Aunt Stella used to say, "I don't want to dirty my real kitchen, it's for show."

Tina was out when we arrived, so we went downstairs and waited for her on the brown, floral, plastic-covered sofa that had been there as long as I could remember. As at my mother's house, Capodimonti cluttered the heavy wooden end tables and sideboards. Ma and Aunt Lina took seats on either side of me and we flipped on the TV. I didn't wonder why Aunt Tina wasn't home, even though we were invited, in fact, I was relieved, and the TV was a welcome distraction from the idle banter of the car ride. No one wanted to really talk about my "problem," though my family overcompensated with food and presence.

About 20 minutes after our arrival, I heard the sound of the front door opening and closing, and Aunt Tina ambled down the stairs. She paused at the landing, gave my mother a knowing glance and started toward the "service" kitchen. Without a greeting or niceties, she said, "Let's go into the bathroom," and plodded onward.

"Come on, Sylvia," Aunt Lina said, hoisting herself up from the sofa.

This is it, I thought. *I've wanted to die for months and now they're going to do the deed.* My heart was pounding as I rose to my feet and followed my elders.

The pink bathroom was dimly lit with candles and filled with the smell of rosemary and lavender. Whatever was happening was premeditated. Aunt Tina shut and locked the door behind us. A shiver ran up my spine. Aunt Lina grabbed me from behind and Ma started gingerly taking off my clothes.

"What are you doing? Are you crazy?" I screamed.

"Just relax, Sylvia," Aunt Lina said calmly, as if this was completely normal.

"It's for your own good, Syl," Ma said matter-of-factly. "The bad spirits have to be taught a lesson."

"Bad spirits? What are you talking about?" I kicked and struggled, but I was, surprisingly, no match for their strength, even at their ages.

"Come on, Sylvia, don't fight," Aunt Lina pleaded. "We are going to fix you."

Stripped to my bra and maternity G-string, I saw the tub. It was filled with filthy brown and green water. Weeds and bits of what I thought was dirt floated on the murky surface.

"Aunt Tina, I think you have a plumbing problem."

"Sylvia, just get in the tub."

"I'm not getting in there! That water is disgusting."

Ma grabbed me around the waist and Lina picked up my legs. Tina held my head as they lowered me down into the freezing, putrid bath. I continued to fight them, but they were of one mind. I was going in that tub.

"Hold your breath, Sylvia," Ma warned, and dunked my head under the water. I came up for air with a yelp and she dunked me again.

"Just hold me under so we can get this over with," I snarled. If *they* killed me, I could still go to heaven.

"Sylvia, just relax. We're not going to let anything bad happen to you," Aunt Tina was taking this very seriously. They all were.

Ma kneeled down next to the tub and swirled the grimy water with her hand, then she took mine. Tina and Lina held hands and Lina linked with Ma. For a moment the room was silent. I closed my eyes and prayed for a quick death. My ears filled with the water, but I could still hear the synchronized breathing of my crazy *famiglia*. As if from nowhere, a quiet chanting that grew louder and louder rose from their circle as they incanted the good spirits. I had no idea what they were saying. Shivering, half naked in the bathtub, I just gave in and waited for the End.

They took turns dunking my head under the dirty water, one by one, kneeling down, like John the Baptist in the River Jordan. I was certain they'd lost their minds. I wanted to call 911, but they had me where they wanted me and I couldn't

Sylvia Lasalandra

escape. I accidentally sucked in a little of the bath and came to my senses, sitting straight up, coughing the shit from my mouth and lungs.

"OK," Aunt Lina said, rising to her feet.

"OK," Aunt Tina echoed.

"OK. The bad spirits, they're gone," my mother said in her broken English. "All the *mal'occhio* trouble you no more."

And then I understood. I had been the matriarch of my family. Even at my young age, I had been a leader and had been admired. Things seemingly came easy for me — success at school, in my career, in my marriage. If I was having problems, there must be bad spirits, *mal'occhio* — the evil eye — keeping me down. And the Witches of Eastwick were going to drive it away.

"The spirits that want you down are gone. Come, we make you a cappuccino."

These women, for all their good intentions, were crazy. Hands reached down and finally pulled me from the water. I had what I later found out was a medley of kitchen herbs brewed in holy water in my hair, in my mouth, in my underwear — everywhere. They dried me, put me in a robe that hung on the back of Aunt Tina's bathroom door and took me into the kitchen for coffee.

"Why don't you offer the evil spirits a cappuccino as they head out the door?" I said, still angry and embarrassed at the invasion of my sense of safety and comfort.

"Aah! Don't make light. They might come back," Aunt Tina admonished.

Of course, what I got out of the evening was a fucking cold, but also a lesson in humility. This thing, this disease, was bigger than me, and no matter how bad things were, I knew my family would never let me go through it alone, or without a fight. If I was going down, we were all going down together, kicking and screaming all the way, trying to stay afloat.

Toetoos

Sixteen

Girlfriends to the Rescue

Keeping loyal friends is like threading beads on a string with
a knot at the end.

—Sylvia Lasalandra, PPD survivor.

They had very different methods, but my girlfriends
were doing all they could to break the postpartum
spell. Marianna and Chip were always willing to step in and
give Ma and Aunt Lina a break from babysitting me. Perhaps
because of the doctor fiascos, or just because she is a terrific
friend, Marianna went above and beyond to help. She would
take me away on little weekend getaways to rejuvenate me.
Once we traveled to Pittsburgh to visit her mom, but most
often she and Chip would whisk me off to the Jersey shore.

One of the first trips was soon after Ma and Papá had taken
Melina. We spent several days trying to relax and enjoy the
last bit of an Indian summer. I was withdrawn, morbid and
inconsolable, but Marianna and Chip sat with me and talked
with me, anything to keep me from myself.

One Sunday afternoon, Marianna left me with Chip while
she went to work, with strict instructions for Chip to keep

me in his sight. We sat on the deck and looked out at the water in silence. The motion of the waves, which normally calmed me, made me fidgety and anxious.

"Chip, I'm going for a walk," I announced.

"Are you sure you're okay, Syl? Why don't you wait until Marianna comes back?"

"I'm fine. I just want to be alone for a little while." I was practically pleading with him. Chip took pity on me.

"Okay. I'll be right here if you need me."

I wandered down the beach to the pier and then to the shops. I didn't know where I was going — in that moment or in my life. The question, *How did I get here?* played over and over in my mind. Nothing made sense. The order of the world was a jumbled mess and I had no idea how to get back to normal.

I milled around like a tourist, going in and out of boutiques and surf shops along the boardwalk. The air was warm and smelled of suntan lotion and briny decay. I fingered skimpy bathing suits and recalled being able to wear one not that long ago. I tried on a pair of sandals in a small clothing shop. They were black platforms, just my style, and they were on sale. My feet were still swollen from the pregnancy, and I tried to squeeze my feet into my usual size 6 to no avail. After several pairs, finally the 7½s fit, until about two weeks later. I still have those sandals and they are still too big.

I had been gone over an hour when I decided I'd had enough shopping. I knew Chip would be worried about me, and Marianna would be furious if she knew I had gone. Chip was preparing dinner when I returned to their condo.

"Marianna called," he said. I knew we were in trouble. "She wants you to call her." I dialed slowly. She answered on the first ring.

"Sylvia, you should not be alone in your condition. If something had happened, I would never forgive myself, or Chip for letting you out of his sight."

"But I'm fine. Nothing happened. Well, I bought shoes." Marianna laughed, her anger and fear subsiding.

"That's my girl. I'll be home for dinner soon. Don't go anywhere. I mean it."

I did feel better after my walk, but the feeling didn't last. In the back of my mind, I knew I had to go home, to go back to Melina, and that terrified me. I just wanted my old life back, but that was impossible.

My closest group of girlfriends and I had gathered a few times since PPD took over my life — the occasional dinner out, Janie's birthday in November — but the first time I was really able to have fun was in February of 2001. Melina was six months old, it was Kelly's birthday and the girls came to me.

We met in the wine tasting room at *Bacchus* — the room I so lovingly painted the day I went into labor with Melina. Surrounded by 700 bottles of wine and an elaborate spread of breads and cheeses, the Fiery Foursome was ready to let go and unwind. Janie, Donna and I raised our glasses to the guest of honor and made a toast: "To health, happiness and friendship."

There was an unspoken agreement to abandon talk of children. Sitting there, looking at my dearest, oldest friends, a wave of happiness swept over me. The old Syl was still in there somewhere and she desperately wanted to come out. The girls were careful not to bring up my situation, but it didn't feel tense or censored. We simply wanted to have fun. They knew I was suffering and they were so happy to see me smile, something I hadn't done in a very long time.

They made me feel wonderful, like I was a good person, a great person and a great friend. No matter how bad things were, I had my friends and they had me. I was coming out and they were ready to help me celebrate my re-entry into life. We laughed and talked, just like old times.

"I feel like a kid again," Kelly said, refilling her glass.

"Well, you're not, birthday girl," Janie laughed.

"I don't care. This is the most fun I've had since we tried to get tattoos."

"Oh, my God. That was so funny," I started laughing.

"Remember Candy, the 300-pound tattoo artist with Bo Derek braids?" Donna reminded us.

"Oh, my God. She hated us," Kelly laughed.

"Yeah, because Sylvia said, 'This is definitely one Candy I would never eat.'"

"Um, Janie, what about you?" I protested. "Rolling around on the floor drunk in your mini-skirt with no underwear on!"

"You made me laugh. I couldn't stand up. At least I didn't steal a giant bowl of chocolate mousse at *somebody's* wedding and eat it in a bathroom stall."

"Oh, my God! Now that was hilarious." We were all laughing as we relived our past antics.

"Janie, it was just sitting there, and they wouldn't let us have it until you said it was okay."

"And the pictures were taking forever." Donna defended us.

"Well, at least you gave it back before you ate it *all*."

Then, out of the blue, Donna blurted out,

"Let's get tattoos!"

"What?"

"For real this time. Let's get matching tattoos. Come on, you guys."

"I'm in," Kelly jumped up.

"Me, too," I said. "Janie?"

"Well, okay. But no peeing on the side of the road this time."

The least drunk of our lot drove the 10-minute stretch to the tattoo parlor. On the short ride, we agreed upon a design: a cluster of grapes. A tight bunch of wine lovers we are. The question that remained was, where?

"How about on our toes? Like on the third one," Kelly suggested. "That way, they're easily hidden, but will look really cute in the summer."

"Oooh! I love it," said Donna.

"Perfect," said Janie.

"Wait a minute." I stopped them. " Janie, I love you, but that means we'll have to look at your wacky feet." Laughter filled the car — Janie does have wacky toes.

"Fuck you, bitch," Janie said with a laugh.

"You can't deny it. Your toes are wacky," I teased.

"Maybe the tattoo will distract the eye from the weirdness," Donna giggled.

"Fine," I said. "Toes it is."

To this day, I think of that night as my coming out party — coming out of the oppression of PPD, back into the world of the living, the really living. No cotillion could have been finer or remembered more fondly. I am connected to these women, not just by friendship — or grape "toetoos" — but also by virtue of my survival. I am alive, and I owe my life to them, and to many others.

The women in my life taught me about devotion. Each one of them offered the best of themselves to get me through. Kelly, who only ever wanted the two children she had, would have adopted Melina to keep her near her real family. Janie and Donna gave of their love and laughter to keep my spirits high and remind me I was human. These precious friends kept me in their sights as I wandered away, making sure I didn't go too far, and, when I was ready, were there with open arms to welcome my return.

After that night, laughter began to creep back into my life, and so did Melina. We still had supervised visits — overnights were still to come — but I was finally starting to feel like a mom. I remembered Melina's christening and the idea of a baby being a miracle. Giving birth to Melina sent me over the edge of despair, but an amazing thing happened to me when I finally looked into her eyes. I realized she *was* my miracle.

Seventeen

Better Than Drugs

I looked at our tiny, perfect creature and it was as though a light switch had been turned on. A great rush of love flooded out of me.

—Madeleine L'Engle, writer and educator.

My family was gathered at my mother's house on a Sunday after church. Johnny was sitting in the armchair holding his daughter Lara. Ma, with Melina in her arms, came over to me on the couch and gingerly laid my baby in my lap. Shuddering, I picked her up and rested her against my shoulder. I knew I should want to hold her, but something still held me back, even after months of struggling to get better.

Suddenly, Melina put her tiny fists on my shoulders and pushed herself up to face me. I tried to avoid her gaze, but Melina just stared straight into my eyes until I looked into hers. She hugged me with those warm blue eyes. In my periphery, I could see Ma and John watching and waiting. Suddenly, everyone in the room disappeared. It was just Melina and me. A flicker of light sparked between us, like a flash of starlight.

"I know you want me to love you," I said to her, and she seemed to understand me. "Okay, baby, I know. I'm trying." I meant it. For the first time, I realized I not only wanted to love her, I did love her.

Melina sighed as if to say, "Finally, you've acknowledged me." She put her little head down on my chest and dropped off to sleep. I knew then that all she wanted was to be loved — not by her grandmother, aunt or father, but by me — and for a moment all the despair left me. I was at last able to embrace the pure love of a mother and child, a love I had never felt before.

Now Melina is my lungs, the air I breathe. She is four years old and the reason I'm alive. It is worth everything I went through when I see her smile, hear her laugh and feel her arms around my neck. The thing that kept me going was the desire to love her the way she deserves, and the hope that I could experience what everyone said was the greatest love a woman can feel. It is. The love I have for Melina is the purest, most refined and truest I have ever experienced. Every day, I hold Melina and laugh with her. I smile at her from across the room and, at every opportunity, I tell her how beautiful she is. But most of all, I tell her how much I love her.

"I love you, Melina. I love you, love you, love you."

"I know, Mommy."

Eighteen

Hills and Valleys

When you are drawing up your list of life's memories, you might place near the top of the list the first moment your baby smiles at you.

—Bob Greene, novelist and columnist.

My journey with postpartum depression did not end there, in fact, it was only the beginning of my recovery. But from that moment, I knew what I was fighting for. As mothers, we are supposed to love our children, help them and care for them, but that tiny baby did all of those things for me just by looking into my eyes. Whenever I need to escape to a place that is true and pure, I recall that instant when I finally understood. It was then that I told myself that I was going to do everything in my power to get better and love her the way a mother should love a child. I wanted her to feel safe in my arms, to let her know that I would always be there for her, to catch her when she falls, to tell her how beautiful she is when she doesn't feel beautiful, but most of all to love her . . . just love her.

. . .

I felt like a traitor leaving Melina with my mother that evening, but we still had many miles to go before we could sleep. I took two tranquilizers in the car to speed the process. Michael and I drove home along Skyline Drive, the treacherous, winding country road I often traveled alone at my most desperate. I was reeling with conflict about what had happened. *She looked at me. She knows I am her mother. But am I ready?*

I had been starting to feel better, able to see Melina more often, even able to laugh a little. This small progress was not lost on Michael. Over dinner with my parents (Ma, as usual, made my favorite dish — eggplant with plum tomato sauce and fresh mozzarella), it was beginning to feel like we were a real family for the first time.

"Syl, honey," he said, negotiating a sharp curve, "don't be afraid to get better."

"What?" I asked, the tightness in my chest returning.

"I know it's hard, but don't be afraid to try. We're here for you and we want you to be well again."

"Look, Michael, I'm not doing this on purpose. I know you want Melina to come home, but I'm still not ready."

"I'm not trying to pressure you, Sylvia. Of course I want Melina home, but I just want you to know that it's okay to feel better."

"But if I feel better, I have to be a mom, and I just can't. Not yet."

"Damn it, that's not what I mean."

"Well, what do you mean?"

"I don't know."

We continued on in silence. I was glad he was driving and

had to concentrate on the road. I wanted him to forget about me. He meant to say, "Don't be afraid to get better, to be who you are again," but I didn't understand. I thought his only concern was Melina, but what he really wished for was for Sylvia to come back to him.

The next day, I was a zombie. Getting better meant facing all the horrible things I had thought and felt about Melina, all of the things I did and did not do for her. I retreated into what had become my regular state of isolation and depression. With every little encouragement Michael would get his hopes up and I would retreat. He tried to understand, but the more he pushed, the more I pulled away.

For every step forward, the guilt of my motherly treason set me back three. *She doesn't deserve me*, I thought, *I'm horrible, ungrateful. There are women all over the world who desperately want a child, but can't have one, and here I am, throwing one away.* With deep calming breaths, I repeated what my mother had told me: "No matter what you are going through, Melina loves you anyway."

As our visits became more frequent, it turned into a game. She would look at me and smile. *Yeah, you're cute*, I would think, *but you're not going to get me*. Echoes of Kelly's words haunted me: "She'll get a hold of you and you won't even know it." And she did.

Getting back to normal

Nineteen

Not Alone

Women suffering PPD need not feel ashamed — it's a real illness! The first step to recovery is being honest with yourself and the people who love you.

—Sylvia Lasalandra, PPD survivor.

Once Melina and I were out of harm's way, an amazing thing happened. People began coming out of the woodwork to share their own stories of postpartum depression. My sister-in-law Lucy and I were on the deck of my mother's house chatting casually when she dropped the first bomb.

"You know, Sylvia," she said quietly, looking out over the backyard, avoiding my eyes, "I've never told anyone this before, but I used to have horrible thoughts of hurting my son when he was a baby."

No one from my husband's family had ever confronted me about my illness, and I was shocked. I thought she always wanted an army of kids instead of the two she had. I was so sad for her.

"Why did you keep it in for all these years?" I asked.

"I was so ashamed."

I knew how she felt. I was afraid to tell anyone about my psychotic thoughts, too. Shame and guilt were keeping us silent; keeping the disease a secret.

Months later, my friend Kelly told me that she also had mild PPD. My friend Marci's paralegal suffered through it as well. Everywhere I turned people were coming out to me, sharing their stories of desperation and shame. Even my own mother had a story.

"Sylvia, remember when Aunt Stella came to visit us after Johnny was born?"

"Sure, Ma."

"Well, I was going through what's happening to you now. The doctors called it a nervous breakdown and exhaustion, but it was the same thing, whatever they call it."

I was stunned.

"What did you do? What was it like?"

"I heard crazy voices in my head. They said we would all be better if I was dead. I wanted to go up to the balcony of our house and jump right off with Johnny in my arms. My sisters saved me, Sylvia. Stella and Tina took care of you and your brothers, even your father. They would not let me alone. They would not let me die. That's why I do what I do. I suffered through this 33 years ago so I could help you today. I didn't understand then, but I understand now. God gave me the strength to survive for me and for you." Tears welled up in my eyes and a stabbing pain shot through my heart.

"Ma, I had no idea."

"Of course you didn't. It was not for you to know."

Everything suddenly made sense. Ma's stubbornness with Michael, his family and the doctors was the direct result of her own experience. She knew exactly what I was going through, and she choreographed my recovery not only be-cause she loved me and wanted me to live, but to make up for lost time.

We may not have known what was happening to our fam-ily during my mother's postpartum depression, but we were affected nonetheless. There was always tension between my father and my brother John. I suspect Papá blamed Johnny for Ma's illness; she was fine before he was born and none of us were ever the same again. My dad and Johnny were not very close growing up, and my mother overcompensated by giving Johnny more attention than the rest of us. In fact, she and John are still very close to this day. Although I know bet-ter now, I felt cheated growing up with the feeling that she loved him more. She didn't love him more, she was making up for the absence, just as I would do with Melina.

Postpartum depression affects 10 to 17 percent of new moth-ers, often those who have children already. It favors no race, age or economic status. It can, and does, happen to anyone at anytime. The cases of psychosis that end in suicide, and oc-casionally infanticide, are more rare, but not as rare as one might think. One in 1,000 women are afflicted every year. The only way these women can be helped is through diag-nosis, proper treatment and compassion.

In other cultures, mothers who have recently given birth are taken care of along with their new babies. In China, for the first month after birth, a new mother is sequestered to her room while her mother, aunts and cousins take on the respon-sibilities of the child. The mother is given time to physically and emotionally recover before she must add the stress of parenting to her burden. In Africa, similar birthing rituals allow the new mother a period of adjustment during which she is pampered and nurtured. In England and Italy, a woman who harms her child due to postpartum psychosis is given treatment, not jail time.

These communities revere and respect motherhood and the birthing process in ways that we do not. They realize that an illness is not a criminal offence. American women are expected to do it all: have children, work full time, have a social life, all while making it look easy. If they can't do it, they are ostracized.

I was at work the evening the Andrea Yates sentencing verdict came down. The TV was on in the noisy bar and, for a moment, I was frozen. My heart seized in my chest. I scooted through the crowd and ran up to my office, locking the door behind me. I flipped on the little TV on the filing cabinet and held my breath.

"Please, God, don't give her the death penalty." I whispered a little prayer. "Please."

I felt like I was on trial myself. I was only a Sicilian mama away from facing the same fate as Andrea Yates. If she'd had the support I was given, her beautiful children would be alive and she would be at home with them. The health care system had already failed her. I couldn't bear it if the justice system did as well.

"Life in prison," the TV reported.

I collapsed on the floor under the weight of my relief. I felt this victory, however small, was a victory for me. Her fate could have been my fate. Her disease was my disease. The Yates verdict was a tiny step in the right direction for our criminal justice system. That she was put on trial at all and not immediately hospitalized was a travesty, but a twinkling of progress shined through.

"Thank you, God," I prayed. "Thank you. On behalf of all women who suffer with PPD, thank you."

When Melina was about five months old, Ma, Lina, Melina and I were waiting in the pediatrician's office for a checkup. There, sitting on the little indoor sliding board among the toys and other waiting children and moms, was a young mother who looked terrified — a look I knew all too well. She was holding a 10-day-old baby. She looked so frightened and alone. Though I was still in the midst of my own terror, I felt compelled to reach out to her. Perhaps emboldened by my own personal support team, I walked over and put my hand on her shoulder.

"It's going to be okay," I whispered. Tears streamed down her face at my words. She looked up at me and I could see her desperation.

"How do you know?"

"I know."

"But I can't do this. I don't want to do this."

"You can. It's ugly, but you'll get through it. You'll get medical help and you'll get through." I didn't want to tell her about my own trouble with doctors. I knew that any discouragement could send her further into the spiral.

"If you want to get in touch with me through the pediatrician, I'm Sylvia, Melina's mom. You can call me anytime."

"Thank you," she said through a half-smile. "You've made me feel 100 times better. I've been feeling so alone."

"I know." She stood up and hugged me. For the first time, I felt a sense of relief and understanding. I didn't know her story, but I knew this woman. She made me feel lucky for the loving family that surrounded me. By giving a little boost of encouragement to this stranger, this sister in pain, I felt encouraged myself.

Every time I remember this woman, I think of the others I have encountered since my recovery. Women will say to me, "I had a friend who went through that," or, "I know some-one who is going through that right now." I can see in their eyes they are talking about themselves. Even when faced with someone who has been through PPD and is talking about it, they still can't bring themselves to say the words. The shame stops here. This book is for the woman on the slide and for all women who are caught in the vise of PPD. We are not alone and we will be silent no longer.

For all of our talk of "family values," the pressures a mother faces are so often trivialized in favor of a romantic ideal of motherhood. This leaves little room for failure and plenty of room for disaster. Maternity leave, only recently made mandatory for our country's workforce, is usually only one month, sometimes two. The pressure on women to snap back immediately after giving birth is not only unrealistic but dangerous — dangerous for the mother and dangerous for the child.

The television airwaves are jammed with ads for "male en-hancement" drugs, and my insurance provider, while offer-ing Viagra and Cialis to any man who wants it, did not cover more than one follow-up visit with my OB/GYN after the birth of my daughter. Bob Dole is not ashamed to proclaim on national television that he can't keep his dick hard, but women who suffer from postpartum depression are too ashamed of being thought of as bad mothers to come forward. Well, I am not ashamed anymore.

The first step in conquering PPD is for women to come forward and say, "Hi, I'm Sylvia and I want to kill my kid." Or at least say, "Hi, I'm Sylvia and I feel like shit. Can someone please help me?" There is no shame in seeking help for any manner of diseases and disorders. PPD should be no different.

The medical community and the legal system do women in this country a great disservice. PPD sufferers are criminalized when they should be medicated; they are imprisoned when they should be hospitalized. Women who suffer through postpartum depression must not be treated as freaks or subhuman beings, but as people who are ill and need help. Cancer, heart disease, AIDS, diabetes are publicly recognized, researched and treated with success. Postpartum depression is no less deadly, nor does it affect society at large any less, yet still, the only time we hear about postpartum depression is when the unthinkable happens.

In 2001, a woman named Melanie Stokes jumped from a 12th-story Chicago hotel window just months after the birth of her first child. Until that day, Melanie's story read like a fairytale: Beautiful, intelligent and successful, both professionally and personally, Melanie was married to the love of her life and belonged to a loving, tight-knit family. But the fairytale ended with the birth of her long-awaited daughter.

Melanie and her husband waited until just the "right" time to start their family, but nothing they did could prepare them for what was to come. Melanie had PPD, but because of the

Melanie Stokes

lack of knowledge among doctors and laypeople, she went untreated, with everyone hoping she would "snap out of it." Melanie struggled with the overwhelming despair that comes with being unable to love and care for a child. Five months after the birth of her daughter, unable to bear the shame of her perceived failure to be a good mother, she checked into a local motel room and jumped out the window.

Melanie's mother, Carol Blocker, continues to lead the fight to raise public awareness of postpartum depression and postpartum psychosis. She lost her precious daughter to an insidious killer, a disease that is curable with the proper diagnosis and treatment. Mrs. Blocker is working with Illinois legislators to pass a bill that will earmark federal funds for research into postpartum depression and psychosis. The last major action on the bill was in February of 2003, when it was referred to the House Subcommittee on Health, and where it remains at the time of this writing. Mrs. Blocker isn't giving up. She addressed the Committee on September 26, 2004, continuing the three-year fight that began with the death of her daughter.

I am aware that I am one of the lucky ones, that Melina is one of the lucky ones. I often think of Melanie Stokes and I wish she were here to tell her own story. Her mother is telling it for her, but it doesn't have a happy ending. In her honor, and the honor of the countless others who anonymously succumbed, I will continue to tell my story to anyone who will listen. I truly believe God gave me this disease because of my big mouth. Before more women fall victim, I will use that big mouth to make sure as many people as possible hear about the dangers of untreated PPD. In the immortal words of Linda Loman from Arthur Miller's "Death of a Salesman," "Attention must be paid." If I can make a difference in one woman's life, in the life of one family, I will have my purpose.

. . .

I have learned on this journey that people fear and hate what they do not understand. Instead of praising my mother and Aunt Lina for taking care of Melina, outsiders directed their confusion at me in often insensitive and hurtful ways. Always masked as concern, I was kicked while I was down by people who professed to care about me. So many times I heard, "You know, Sylvia, a baby really belongs with its mother." Well, I believe a baby belongs where it is safe and can be cared for properly. I couldn't understand why no one was just happy the baby was okay. The judgments and hostilities I faced should not have been surprising to me, given the way women with postpartum are perceived by society at-large.

PPD is a very misunderstood illness, but with all the attention on depressive disorders in the last 15 years, it's a mystery to me why it remains out of the public discourse. We all need to be educated about the early warning signs and proper courses of action so that immediate intervention can prevent not only the extreme cases of suicide and homicide, but also the destruction of families through isolation and neglect.

Over the summer, I watched coverage of the Democratic National Convention. Just the name alone scares me— DNC. It makes me want to cross my legs and not let anything near my vagina. Scarier still is that the City of Boston spent $50 million on security for a man who wasn't even our president, and our government can't spend $1 to fund research into treatments for PPD. These kinds of statistics blow my mind. It angers me to think that if PPD were a male disorder, more money would be devoted to research, education and treatment. Viagra, for crying out loud, is readily available and fully covered by insurance for any man who wants it. The same cannot be said for birth control. Billions of dollars per year are funneled into research to fight diseases, the development of new drugs and to healthcare, and still a disease as destructive to families as PPD flies under the radar.

The changes must start with the medical community. Doctors should be aware of the warning signs and able to diagnose a depressed mother. Nurses, who are on the front lines, should be better equipped to recognize women who are feeling more "blue" than usual. Those women should be flagged for follow-up before they are discharged from the hospital. If only the nurse that discharged me had listened to my concerns. If only I had been given an emergency number to call if I felt suicidal or had thoughts of harming my baby, I would not have suffered to the extreme that I did.

These safeguards can prevent the preventable and can be easily implemented. My insurance provider only covered one follow-up visit with my OB/GYN after the birth of my daughter, and because it was a Caesarian birth, the doctor was really only concerned about my incision. I needed a referral from my GP in order to see a psychiatrist, and, even then, the insurance company limited the number of visits. If doctors dismiss the symptoms of PPD as hormonal ravings, how are lay people supposed to take it seriously? Psychiatric obstetrics and gynecology, still a burgeoning field, should be available to all women who need it.

Postpartum depression can occur anytime within the first two years after the birth of a child and, left untreated, can manifest itself into postpartum psychosis and a detachment from reality. If the same attention were placed on treating PPD as is making sure men can do their part in making those babies in the first place, thousands of women a year would be spared the suffering that I, and so many others, have endured.

. . .

Recently, I sat in the stands watching my daughter play soccer with the other 3 to 6-year-olds. I was talking to another mom sitting next to me, watching her boys play. Actually, she was talking to me and she wouldn't shut up. She had overheard me telling Michael on the cell phone about my progress on the book and, as I hung up the phone, she interrupted me.

"I'm sorry for eavesdropping, but . . . ," I knew at that point I was doomed, ". . . I'm a psychologist and I think I can help you."

I wanted to say, "You people couldn't help me in 2000, what makes you think you can help me now?" but I held my tongue.

I sat quietly, nodding and smiling, and listened to her drone on, spewing psychobabble. I told her about the problems with the psychiatrist and psychologist.

"That is a shame," she said, "but to this day, not many healthcare practitioners really understand how to treat PPD. I am treating a woman who is now institutionalized because her disease went untreated for so long."

She kept going on and on. I just kept nodding and smiling, hoping to myself that she wasn't going to charge me for the session. The kids came running up for their 2-minute water break. I gave Melina her water and told her what a good job she was doing. When the coach blew the whistle, she ran back onto the field excitedly and then stopped, turned and said "Mommy, please don't leave." I assured her that I wouldn't.

The psychologist turned to me and said, "Do you know why she said that? Why she is scared? It's because you left her when she was a newborn and weren't there for her." I could not believe my fucking ears. I wanted to turn around and punch this woman and wrestle her to the ground, but we were at a soccer game, not a wrestling match.

"I have enough guilt to last me a lifetime, thank you very much, and plenty inner demons involving this issue. It's a shame people like you have a degree to fuck with people's minds." She looked shocked and embarrassed and kept her opinions to herself until the end of the game, when she apologized.

Even though I knew I did the best for Melina that I could, and have spent the subsequent years trying to make it up to her, the psychologist's words bothered me that whole weekend. If a mental health professional can't see the harm in her offhand diagnosis, how can we hope to reach the rest of the population? The answer is, compassion and education. If only I had known, in my darkest days, that I was not alone, that others had survived this terrifying disease before me, I may not have struggled for quite so long. In my quest for knowledge and healing, I only wanted to be told that I wasn't a monster. Underinformed doctors were helpless to provide me the care I required. My friends and family tried to make me understand, but were afraid to share their own experiences. Their own shame kept them silent.

There is no need for shame. Postpartum depression and postpartum psychosis are illnesses. With the proper treatment, they can be overcome. It is for no other reason that I am sharing my story — to end the cycle of shame and silence. Our society paints afflicted women as monsters. I want these women, all women, to know that they are human.

Melina at age three and a half

Twenty

My Miracle

One thing about having a baby is that each step of the way, you simply cannot imagine loving him more than you already do, because you are bursting with love, loving as much as you are humanly capable of — and then you do love him even more.

—Anne Lamott, writer.

I'll never be able to make up for the time I was absent from Melina's life, but I will continue to try. I know now that I did the best for her that I could. By giving her up to my parents' care, I made sure she had everything she needed and, as parents, that's what we are supposed to do. Feeling guilt and shame helps no one, it only gets in the way of recovery. I want people to know that there is no shame in post-partum depression. There is no reason for guilt.

Melina has so much fun with her father, grandparents, cousins and aunts and uncles, the people who were around her most in her infancy, but she still wants to be with me. We have a special bond and a unique understanding, because we survived postpartum depression together. With the help of my little girl, I went 12 rounds and I kicked postpartum's ass.

The week before Thanksgiving in 2004, Michael, Melina and I joined my parents at their condominium in Florida. Although we always enjoy our time at the beach, this trip was particularly special for me. It's been three years since the beginning of my recovery. It was a long, arduous journey, but I survived. We sold our restaurants in 2003 so we could spend more time with Melina. People thought we were crazy, but I have a saying: "You can't fall in love with bricks and mortar." You *can* fall in love with a beautiful four-year-old girl who already wishes she was twenty-five.

The divided path that Michael and I took as we journeyed through recovery came together at last. He had both his girls back and we were finally a family. We missed the first year of her life and we refused to miss anymore. The three of us had a lot of lost time to make up.

I watched Melina playing along the shore from the gazebo. *There she is*, I thought, *with her 'Little Mermaid' bathing suit crawling up her butt, those big toes she inherited from Michael digging into the sand*. She was collecting seashells and shrieking with laughter as Michael chased her along the surf. *That's my little girl, my little savior.*

I remember sitting in that very same gazebo just four

years earlier contemplating the end. And here I am with a new beginning. The despair is gone and I am left with joy.

Instead of hours of desolate, petrified silence, the gazebo is filled with songs and stories and laughter. I made it. Melina made it. We made it.

Melina's love is like a drug, and because of her restorative effects, I am alive. When I look into her eyes, I can see what she will be. She is everything. She is the only person that makes me feel complete. Although I have had material success, more than I ever dreamed of, my life is richer because of my daughter.

As I get ready to go into the city to have lunch with friends, Melina watches me.

"Have fun, mommy. Don't drive too fast," she says.

"OK, baby," I laugh as I kiss her goodbye. "I love you, Melina. I love you, love you, love you."

"I know, Mommy."

She knows.

Afterword and Resources

When I was sick, there were so few resources at my disposal. My closest family and friends were all I had — to my great joy and gratitude — but not everyone has that luxury. As people begin to understand what PPD is and how it can be successfully treated, women, their children and the people who love them can be spared the agony of silent suffering. We can make a difference through education. Approximately 10 to 17 percent of women experience postpartum depression — 10 to 17 percent! — and those are just the reported cases. But the word is getting out. Women are demanding to be heard and to be understood. Cases like Andrea Yates' and Melanie Stokes' should not exist, and they can be prevented the better we educate ourselves.

With hormones raging, thoughts turn to the realization that life is changing forever; it's no wonder that many women experience fear and apprehension. Had my nurses been educated about the realities of PPD, I could have been diagnosed and treated much sooner. The fact that I came out the other side and have been able to repair and have a positive relationship with my daughter is nothing short of a miracle. I had no real medical treatment. I had no real psychiatric support from the doctors I enlisted for help. I only had the love and support of my family, while self-medicating all along the way. It's not the ideal course of treatment, and I do not recommend it for others. That's why I'm telling my story. No one should have to beg her doctors for help. No one should have to be subjected to the judgmental stares and comments from those who fear the unknown. Every woman who suffers from PPD should be heard.

The Warning Signs — A PPD Primer

"Baby Blues" occurs in about 80 percent of mothers, usually appearing during the first week after the birth of the child, and can last up to three weeks. The symptoms are moodiness, irritability, lack of concentration, sadness, anxiety and feelings of dependency. This, too, shall pass . . .

Postpartum Depression occurs in about 10 to 17 percent of mothers. Generally, symptoms will arise in the first days after the birth, but they can appear anytime in the first two years after the birth of the child and can last as long. Because of the prevalence of the baby blues, doctors are reluctant to diagnose PPD in the first weeks. Symptoms include loss of appetite, insomnia, restlessness and fatigue.

Postpartum Psychosis occurs in 1 percent of mothers, usually stemming from untreated postpartum depression. The symptoms include suicidal and even homicidal impulses. Women often experience auditory and visual hallucinations. These can trigger dangerous behavior, putting the lives of the mother and the baby at risk.

Sylvia Says

The *Do*s and *Don't*s of Helping a Woman with PPD

Say

You are not alone.

We are here for you.

We will get through this
together.

Please let me help you –
I can clean the house, talk,
listen, stay over. Anything

This is temporary. You will
get well.

The baby will be fine,
just worry about yourself.

This isn't your fault.

I love you.

Don't Say

Just relax.

Why are you so down?
Look at everything you have.
You should be overjoyed.

Try to snap out of it.

Maybe you should take
some medication.

Just think positive.

Do you know how many
women would love to have
a baby and can't?

I don't know why you are
making such a big deal.
It's just a baby.

Women have been having
babies for centuries.
You are overreacting.

Sylvia's Carte Blanche

I, Sylvia Lasalandra, give permission to any woman suffering
PPD to kick in the balls any asshole who says anything from
the *Don't Say* list. If they don't have balls, then you have my
permission to slap the bitch.

A Recommendation

The best book I came across in my preparation to tell my own story was *Beyond the Blues* by Shoshanna S. Bennett, Ph. D. and Pec Indman, Ed. D., MFT, published by Moodswings Press in 2003. If only I had this resource when I was suffering PPD! Not only does *Beyond the Blues* provide valuable facts and treatment recommendations, it includes case studies of real women, like me, who suffered and survived. If I had been able to read this book when Melina was still an infant, I am convinced my journey would have been much shorter. It told me more than any doctor ever did. I could have seen with my own eyes that I wasn't crazy. I was sick, sure, but I was not alone.

When I discovered *Beyond the Blues* at the library, I thought, *This is great. The word is getting out there,* but when I went to my local Barnes and Noble to get my own copy, they didn't carry it. I was shocked. Off I traipsed to the Borders I had visited in my desperate PPD days. It wasn't there either. Both places offered to order the book for me, but come on! A desperate woman seeking answers should not have to wait for help. This book, while still not readily available, should be in the same category as *What to Expect When You're Expecting*, which is on every mother-to-be's shelf. I read that book and there was no mention of postpartum depression. It should be called, *Let's Not Talk About the Bad Stuff That Can Happen When You're Expecting.*

This disease is real. It's as real as cancer and diabetes and the common cold. The difference is that it is curable. Recognition, treatment and support are all a woman needs to overcome postpartum depression before it spirals into psychosis.

Below you will find a list of resources that I came across in my ongoing research to raise awareness about postpartum depression. If you or someone you love are reading this book and recognize your loved one or yourself in these pages, I implore you to get help now. Time is the only thing that is not on your side.

As I've said before, God gave me this disease because I have a big mouth, and I won't shut up until I am heard. No longer should women suffer silently in shame. Together, we can kick postpartum's ass.

The Laundry List

Books

Beyond the Blues by Shoshanna S. Bennett, Ph. D. and Pec Indman, Ed. D., MFT, Moodswings Press, 2003

Sleepless Days: One Woman's Journey Through Postpartum Depression, by Susan Kushner Resnik, St. Martin's Press, 2000

This Isn't What I Expected by Karen Kleiman and Valerie Raskin, Bantam Books, 1994

The Postpartum Husband by Karen R. Kleiman, Xlibris Corporation, 2001

Online Resources

Support Groups

Postpartum Support International
http:www.postpartum.com

Depression After Delivery
http:www.depressionafterdelivery.com

Articles

"Beyond the Baby Blues" by Kathleen Doney
http:www.healthfinder.gov/news/newsstory.asp?docID=519021

"Descent into Darkness: Depression" (part 1 of 2), Louise
Kiernan, Chicago Tribune, Chicago, IL, February 16, 2003
http:www.chicagotribune.com

Informational Sites

The Stokes Foundation
(332) 225-1310
http:www.melaniesbattle.org

4Women.gov
The National Women's Health Information Center
http:www.4women.gov/faq/postpartum.htm

To contact Sylvia Lasalandra,
learn more about the short film
A Daughter's Touch,
or order copies of this book,
please contact:
adaughterstouch@aol.com
or visit:
www.adaughterstouch.com

A Daughter's Touch
by Sylvia Lasalandra
SOFTCOVER · 5.5" x 8.5" · 208 PAGES
ISBN 0-9764867-0-x
QUATTRO M PUBLISHING

Discounts available for reading groups
and non-profit organizations